the power that keeps them aloft they all gave the same answer.

God.

That's right, they said their power for living came from a personal relationship with God. Unlike the Spaceship Columbia which was put aloft by man's efforts, they all said they had tried man's way and found it empty. But when they turned to God, and allowed Him to take control of their lives, they began to soar.

"God?" you say. "Well, He might be able to help folks who already have made it. But what about me?"

Wait a minute. God is not just for the famous, or the rich, or those nice folks who dress up to go to church or the synagogue. God is for everyone. He loves those who are helpless. He loves the alcoholics, the drug addicts, those who have lost power and are tumbling end over end in space, headed for a sure crack-up (unless they burn out first on re-entry). He loves the fellow who's out of work, the housewife caught in the web of adultery, the lonely teenager, the frustrated businessman.

He loves you. And if you will let Him, He will not only direct your path, but will give you power to live.

D0002122

That's what this book is all about. Power for living. A long time ago the prophet Isaiah discovered this. What he wrote has been tested by millions of people from all walks of life, across the years. Now it's your time to test it, too, and let

God give you power, not only to live but to live abundantly. Here's what Isaiah said: *"Those who hope in the Lord will renew their strength. They will soar on wings like eagles; they will run and not grow weary, they will walk and not be faint"* (Isaiah 40:31).

Jamie Buckingham
Melbourne, Fla.

"In everything you do, put God first,
and he will direct you and crown your
efforts with success."
Proverbs 3:6 (The Living Bible)

REACHING YOUR GOAL

Everyone dreams of success. It is their goal, or destination, in life.

Some see success as making a lot of money, living comfortably, and retiring easy.

Others dream of becoming proficient in their field, making money, and having folks look up to them as important and wise.

Still others see success as the accumulation of material things—without debt. Owning your own house, driving an expensive car, being able to walk into the store and buy anything you want. That's success.

Then there are those who equate success with having a happy family: a loving wife or husband and obedient children.

To others success is long life, free from disease and heartache.

Everyone has a dream of success.

The Bible says that if you *"delight yourself in the Lord He will give you the desires of your heart"* (Psalm 37:4). That's a marvelous promise. The problem, it seems, is that it seldom happens. I mean, if it did it seems many would be healthy, wealthy and wise—for that's what we desire, isn't it?

Why then, aren't we successful—if that's the desire of our heart?

Could it be that we have a wrong idea of what success is? Is it possible we haven't listened to God's conditions for success?

The first condition listed—indeed, the only condition listed—is to "delight yourself in the Lord." In other words, put God first. Jesus said the same thing when He told His disciples that if they would *"seek first God's kingdom and God's righteousness,"* everything else necessary for life would be given them as well. (Matt. 6:33)

Our problem is not that we don't have goals. Our problem is having the wrong goals.

GETTING OFF AT THE WRONG PLACE

Last year I boarded a plane in New York to fly to my home in Melbourne, Florida. The plane made one stop en route at Tampa before flying on to Melbourne. Since we were running behind schedule the stewardess asked all the Melbourne passengers to remain on the plane during the brief stop in Tampa.

I was busy reading and didn't pay much attention to what was going on, but I began to realize we had been on the ground in Tampa much longer than usual. I asked one of the flight attendants what was wrong.

"We've lost two of our Melbourne passengers," she said. "They accidentally got off here in Tampa and we haven't been able to find them and get them back on the plane."

In a few minutes two elderly women came rushing aboard the plane. They were obviously flustered and speaking rapid Italian to each other, complete with hand gestures. The stewardess got them buckled in, and we immediately took off for the short flight across the state to Melbourne.

After we were aloft the stewardess stopped by my seat and told me what had happened. The two women were from Italy. They spoke no English. This was their first trip to the United States. They were visiting family members who lived in the Melbourne area—and who were waiting for them at the Melbourne airport. It was the biggest trip of their lives and they were excited—and a little scared.

They had boarded in Rome for the long flight to the United States, then changed planes in New York for the flight south to Melbourne. Since they could not understand English they did not realize the domestic flight made a stop in Tampa before flying on to Melbourne. When the plane landed in Tampa and they looked out the window and saw palm trees waving in the Florida sun, they assumed they had reached their destination. They joined the crowd getting off in Tampa and hurried off the plane looking for their loved ones who had promised to meet them at the airport.

What they failed to realize was that they were 120 miles short of their goal. They had gotten off in Tampa thinking their dream of a lifetime was at last fulfilled, only to discover they were lost in a huge airport with no loved ones to meet them.

The flight attendants finally found them, wandering dazed through the strange terminal. But when they tried to convince them to get back on the plane, they refused. They mistakenly thought they were going to be sent back to their home country. Someone finally found a baggage handler who spoke Italian. He explained they were not where they were supposed to be. Only then did the women rush back on the plane, eager to go on to their final destination.

Most of us are like that. For some reason—maybe it's because we don't understand God's language in the Bible—we get off at the wrong destination. We equate money, security, and prestige with success. We don't understand that true success is found in having our *spiritual* needs met. Few of us ever arrive at that ultimate success because we are too busy rushing through the airport of material success.

What are the things that cause you to get off in Tampa when your real need is to go to Melbourne?

There could be a lot of reasons. Maybe you don't understand the language. What you need is an interpreter. Someone to come along and explain God's directions.

Or maybe someone gave you bad directions. There are a lot of folks wandering around who seem to delight in misleading people these days. That's one of the reasons we've given you this book—to help you find your way, to encourage you to get on the right plane—the one which will take you to *real success*.

Perhaps you've been blinded by the sight of palm trees. All your life you've lived in the mountains and just the sight of what seems like success is so good you've decided to stop at the first watering hole, rather than going on to discover God's best.

Maybe in your eagerness to find success, you've listened to someone who's offered you an easy way, and you have settled for some false religion.

Maybe you followed the crowd. After all, there are more people getting off in Tampa than Melbourne, so why not go where everyone else seems to be going.

Or perhaps you're just afraid. You've heard all sorts of stories about people who followed God, who put their trust in Him. You don't want to become a fanatic, so you'll just spend your life in the Tampa airport, riding the escalators and looking out the windows at the waving palm trees.

Sound silly?

Sound familiar?

EIGHT WHO HAVE FOUND SUCCESS

Maybe it would help if I introduced you to some folks who didn't allow worldly success to blind them from finding God's goal of success. This kind of success is a lasting success that no one can take away from them.

Roger Staubach

FOOTBALL SUPERSTAR

For a number of years Roger Staubach was the most successful quarterback in the National Football League. His years with the Dallas Cowboys made his name a household word among sports fans all over the world. You might think Roger would list his success with the Cowboys as the most important thing in his life. But in his own words, that's not true.

"Ours is a very dynamic, fast-paced world. Sometimes your mind seems to spin when you consider everything that is happening. It seems that it's just one thing after another, that you just can't enjoy peace of mind these days.

"To me, there's a very simple solution. If you have a relationship with Jesus Christ, He will give you peace of mind.

"My future reaches far beyond football, and this really excites me. Christianity is the most important part of my life.

"If we live for God and not for ourselves, we'll be able to withstand anything in life. If only we'd try to live beyond the earthly life we're involved in every day, there wouldn't be problems like war, adultery, prejudice, and crime."

Roger has a verse of Scripture he says sums up success for him. *"Since we have been justified through faith, we have peace with God through our Lord Jesus Christ."* (Romans 5:1)

Steve Bartkowski
QUARTERBACK FOR THE ATLANTA FALCONS

Steve Bartkowski of the Atlanta Falcons is one of the top quarterbacks in the National Football League. In fact, many sports experts call him the best pure passer in pro football today. He has twenty team records to his credit, and has been to the Pro Bowl twice.

You might think that football was the most important thing in Steve Bartkowski's life, but it isn't.

"Of course I love playing football," he says, "and despite the pressures of the game, there is a great thrill that goes along with being quarterback for a professional football team. But, there is no greater attainment than to know God in a personal way. Nothing compares to it in all the world. As for my career, I leave that in His hands. It says in His Word: 'In everything you do, put God first, and He will direct you and crown your efforts with success.' (Proverbs 3:6).

"For years the Bible was a dead book to me . . . like grits without salt. But after I gave my life to Jesus Christ, it became alive. I saw that the Bible was God's way of talking to me.

"If anyone has experienced success in life, I have. I've had money, fame and athletic achievement. I've pretty much seen it all and done it all, and I've found that it isn't worth anything without Jesus Christ in control of my life."

Here's a statement from a woman known as "America's Sweetheart"—an Olympic medalist who later became the highest-paid female athlete in history.

Janet Lynn

OLYMPIC ICE SKATING CHAMPION

When I was 11 years old, I asked Christ to help me live. From that time on He has consistently been there when I needed a friend as well as being an everpresent guiding force in my life.

"My faith has often been challenged as an ice skater and also as a person. Though I'm not great at being patient, Christ has worked good out of situations I would have never believed He could.

"In 1972 I really wanted to win the Gold Medal in the Olympics in Sapporo, Japan, but found myself in a seemingly hopeless fourth place after compulsories. I gave the final performance as an offering to Christ. Now, 11 years later, that performance is still very much remembered by the Japanese people. I received the Bronze Medal instead of the Gold, but that performance has afforded me many other opportunities.

"Later, God seemed to abruptly take away my skating career because of asthma. In its place He gave me a wonderful husband and three precious sons and and a broader view of the world. And after six years, my work and His power gave me back my skating career as well.

"Now, my family and I try to seek God in what we do. We are doing that by being involved in a church and studying the Bible with a group of other Christian people."

Charles W. Colson

FORMER COUNSEL TO THE
PRESIDENT OF THE UNITED STATES

"I felt a strange deadness when I left the White House. I'd gotten to the top of the mountain, and I couldn't think of any other mountains.

"And then I saw Tom Phillips, an old friend, a guy much like myself. By age 40 he had become president of a large corporation—a fantastic success story. When I saw him in the spring of '73, he seemed totally different—less frantic. He was smiling, he was radiant, caring about me. What had happened? He'd committed his life to Jesus Christ.

"The whole idea of an intelligent, educated, successful businessman, saying, 'I've accepted Him and committed my life,' just threw me. Months went by. Then one evening Tom read me the chapter on pride in C. S. Lewis' *Mere Christianity*. It was a torpedo.

"My biggest problem had always been intellectual reservations. I knew there was a God, but I could never see how man could have a personal relationship with Him. Then the case for Christ became obvious. That night I experienced a feeling of tremendous cleansing, of wholeness, as I accepted Jesus Christ as my Lord and Saviour."

Even though Charles Colson paid for his sins by going to prison, he is not a failure. He has found success for living through Jesus Christ. He has told the story in his best-selling books, *Born Again*, and *Life Sentence*. By his life he has proved that real success is not found by being in the White House, nor can it be taken away by being sentenced to the Big House. Success is found in a relationship with Jesus Christ.

Wallace Johnson

CO-FOUNDER OF HOLIDAY INNS

"I've had a lot of successes and my share of trials. I've worked long and hard, often as much as 16 hours a day, under some trying circumstances. Through them all, I've learned that the only answer to problems—and to the future of the world—is having a personal relationship with Jesus Christ.

"The only people who are truly happy are those who have found Jesus.

"The one reason why we've always had an open Bible in every room in the Holiday Inn motels is to help people find Jesus and the solution to their problems, no matter who they are.

"I could reminisce about how that open Bible has saved thousands. Once a man from Mobile, Alabama, who had some business reversals, packed a gun and drove to Birmingham with the intention of killing himself. When he

checked into a Holiday Inn and found the open Bible in his room, he read it and found Christ.

"Personal problems, social problems—whatever the problem—the solution is found in knowing Christ. I know He's made the difference in my life. Why not in yours?"

Edward L. Johnson
A LEADER IN THE SAVINGS & LOAN INDUSTRY

"As retired Chief Executive Officer of Financial Federation, Inc., I've had to determine what's good and what's bad for the business. I felt the responsibility for handling a hundred million dollars in value that belong to stockholders. That demanded uncompromising standards and all the business acumen I had.

"I don't go around waving a flag, but I make no bones about it—I seek and receive God's help in my business. Success, for me, means being in the will of God. That's the kind of success which is eternal—not subject to the whims of a changing economy. The Scriptures say that the one who does the will of God abides forever. I believe that and I live by that.

"One of the things that made an impact on my life was when someone said to me, 'Your mother prayed for you before you were born.' She died when I was only 3, and I committed my life to Christ when I was 17. I've gone on and trusted the Lord ever since. His help is a constant reality in every facet of my life: at home, in church, in sorrow, in joy. Why shouldn't it work in business?"

Arthur S. DeMoss

INSURANCE COMPANY FOUNDER
AND EXECUTIVE

"Shortly before my 25th birthday, I was tens of thousands of dollars in debt. This in spite of the fact that I'd been working over 100 hours a week.

"Like so many other businessmen, I had the peculiar notion that I was indispensable to my business. If I had to leave it even a few hours, I'd call the office frequently just to make sure everything was all right.

"When I gave my life to Jesus Christ, He promised to lift my burdens, meet all my needs, and solve my problems. He first took me out of debt right after my conversion. I no longer had to work night and day and Sundays.

"What did I do? I put God first. The more time and money I gave Him, the more He gave me. Now I spend time every day reading the Bible and praying for God's guidance. I've given God my business and any problems that come up. Some might say it's incredible, but it's true—I never worry any more."

Art DeMoss discovered that success for living came through peace with God. Money and fortune were his also, but none of this was as important as the peace of mind which he found through Jesus Christ. That's real power for living.

Now let me introduce you to a final friend, a man who is not only an outstanding athlete but a sharp businessman as well. Known as "Dr. J.", he was acclaimed the most valuable basketball player in the NBA in 1981. But his real power does not come from his strong legs nor is it found in his muscular arms and shoulders which enable him to dunk the ball with either hand. Here's his secret for power for living.

Julius ("Dr. J.") Erving

NBA BASKETBALL STAR

"At age 29 I realized I was looking good on the outside but was hitting a lot of peaks and valleys on the inside. After searching for the meaning of life for over ten years, I found the meaning in Jesus Christ.

"When I gave my life to Jesus Christ, I began to understand my true purpose for being here. It's not to go through life and experience as many things as you possibly can and then turn to dust and be no more. The purpose of life is to be found through having Christ in your life and understanding what His plan is and following that plan.

"Now, there's no pressure in my life, and I'm never alone. I know that my Christian faith has helped me put my priorities in order. If I put God number one and my family after that, along with my social existence and my job, I can withstand any attack, and criticism.

"Since I asked Christ to be my Lord and Saviour, there are still some peaks and valleys, but I am being operated on by the greatest Doctor of them all, so that glory goes to Him."

There you have it . . . the words of eight who made it to real success. These are people who didn't get off the plane at the wrong stop.

Did you notice what they had in common? All realized they were failures without God—even though all were quite successful by this world's standards. They all had a personal relationship with Jesus Christ and a profound respect for the Bible as the Word of God.

You ask, "But how does this apply to me?"

I've shared their lives with you for one reason—to let you know that you, too, can find power for living. That's what this book is all about. So I encourage you to read on. We've just begun to share with you how you can reach the right destination . . . how you can change your life and reach the goal of real success—a goal which God wants you to reach, also.

So if you've gotten off the plane at the wrong stop—or maybe taken the wrong flight altogether—then this book is for you. The desires of your heart can be met. You can find power for living.

And God said, Let us make man in our
image after our likeness: and let them
have dominion over the fish of the sea,
and over the fowl of the air, and over
the cattle, and over all the earth, and
over every creeping thing that creepeth
upon the earth.

Genesis 1:26 *(KJV)*

YOU ARE SPECIAL TO GOD

There is a legend among the Cheyenne Indians of an isolated village on the edge of a forest. For years the adults in the village had practiced a little routine. One by one they would sneak out of the village and follow a small path through the forest to a silver stream. There was a log over the stream which had been worn smooth by many moccasined feet. Looking around to make sure no one was looking, the Indian would walk out on the log. Looking down into the silver stream, he would see his reflection. Then, in a quiet voice, he would begin to talk. He would tell the stream all the deep things of his heart. Doing this made him feel good. When he was finished he would return to the village.

Even though all the adult Indians did this on a regular basis, they never told anyone. However, everyone seemed to know everyone else was doing the same thing.

One day two Indian children found the path into the woods. Curious, they followed it and soon found the silver stream. Seeing the log over the stream, they walked out on it and looked down. There, in the water, they saw the reflection of their faces. Before long they were talking to the stream, telling it all the deep things of their hearts. It made them feel good. Very good.

Running down the path, they entered the village and called the adults together. But when they told the adults what they had discovered, and what they had done, the adults were offended—and threatened. They took up stones and chased the children out of the village.

The meaning of the legend, according to the Cheyenne, is that everyone needs someone to talk to, someone to relate to, someone to whom you can tell all the deep things of your heart. But since that is also considered a sign of weakness, you dare not let anyone else know.

The Indians are half right. We are created with a deep need to relate. Someone once said that inside every man is a little boy still trying to please his father. I guess the same thing applies to the little girl who resides inside every woman. Inside all of us is a child who desperately needs to lean on God.

But our society has done a strange thing. It has conditioned us to look upon dependence on God as a sign of weakness. We see "success" as the ability to go it alone, to make it without anyone's help—especially God's help. Therefore when we hear someone say, "I surrendered to God," or "I asked Jesus to take control of my life," we immediately think of the person as a weakling, a washout, a failure who couldn't make it on his own and had to call on God for help.

This is basically a western concept, by the way. Most people in Third World nations, and nearly all those who live in the East, see dependence on the "spirit world" as a natural part of living. It's only Europeans and Americans, with our strong sense of independence, who are reluctant to call upon God for help. Yet, like the Indians, when we get alone and are honest—standing on the log looking down into the silver stream, there is a strong urge to speak the deep things of our heart. And when we do, we feel good inside; for inside every human being there is a small voice which whispers, telling us despite what the world says, God loves us and we are special to Him.

Our problem is pride. We don't want to admit that we're incapable of handling life's problems alone.

Charlie Brown is constantly struggling with this. One day Charlie was talking to his friend, Linus, about the pervasive sense of inadequacy he feels all the time. "You see, Linus," Charlie moaned, "it goes all the way back to the beginning. The moment I was born and set foot on the stage of life they took one look at me and said, 'Not right for the part.' "

How many of us, like Charlie Brown, have looked in the mirror and concluded we were "not right for the part."

It was Charlie who complained to Linus about his publisher. "The publisher sent me a rejection slip," lamented Charlie.

"So what?" said Linus. "Lots of writers get rejection slips."

"But I didn't even submit a manuscript," cried Charlie.

It's that kind of feeling which can quickly turn into an attitude—the attitude of rejection and inadequacy. But this is a perversion of the truth. It is a lie, constantly whispered to us by the devil, to convince us we are really not created in the image of God, that we are not precious to God, that even though Jesus Christ may have died on a cross, He didn't do it for me. If the lie is not corrected, if the attitude is not checked, it could easily lead to depression or worse.

Cartoonists are constantly playing on this aspect of life. In Al Capp's comic strip, " 'Li'l Abner," there was a strange little character who had a dark cloud which hung over his head and accompanied him everywhere. As a result, wherever this pathetic little fellow went there were disasters which followed. Trucks ran off bridges. Pianos fell out of skyscrapers. People dropped into open manholes. We used to laugh at this poor, little Joe, but only because we saw ourselves in him.

Many in today's world feel they live under such a curse. It is like a dark shadow which is always with them. Eventually, they feel, it will catch up with them and consume them.

The fact is, that's not too far from wrong. The Bible tells us that all men are "sinners"; that is, they are trying to live apart from God and His laws. This leads to a deep separation from God. As a result, since all good things come from God, it is difficult for the natural man to experience anything of lasting good.

King David, who had just had a good look at himself when the prophet Nathan came along and pointed out some evil things in his life, confessed an eternal truth when he said, *"Surely I have been a sinner from birth, sinful from the time my mother conceived me"* (Psalm 51:5).

That's a powerful confession, and one that is profoundly true. In other words, David took a good look at himself and said, "Not right for the part."

If we were to diagram this we'd do it by making a chart with lines extending out in all directions saying, "I'm not okay," "You're not okay," "We're not okay," "They're not okay," "It's not okay."

Now if you had not been a "sinner from birth," then you could change that to say, "I'm okay, you're okay, we're all okay, and everything's dandy."

But that's not the way it is according to the Bible. The fact is *"All have sinned and fallen short of the glory of God"* (Romans 3:23).

It is this "sin" which separates us from God and keeps us from being the success God intends for us to be. Therefore, before we do anything else, we need to take care of the *sin problem* in our lives.

Maybe it will be easier to understand if I describe it in terms of a man with his golf club. In the hands of a skilled golfer, a golf club can be used to knock a ball from the tee down the fairway, onto the green, and into the cup. But that's not possible if the golf club has been misused. Say it's been used to pry open the garage door, or maybe your son left it in the gutter and it was run over by the garbage truck. Now the head is cracked open and the shaft is bent so it looks like a Z. No matter how much the golfer wants to use it in the tournament, he'll never be able to play golf using that club.

That's what sin does to our lives. It makes us unusable. It causes us to give in to defeat and say, "So what. Forget about it. Tomorrow you die anyway. So eat, drink, and sleep with Mary."

But even though King David got honest with himself and recognized he was a sinner, he didn't stop there. He called out to God for cleansing and asked God to create in him a pure heart. In short, he did what those men in Chapter One did—he asked God to *"wash away all my iniquity and cleanse me from my sin"* (Psalm 51:2).

You see, we all have a choice. To live God's way—or to live our way. In Chapter One we met some men who said they had decided to follow Jesus. Although successful by the world's standards, they admitted they could not make it alone. Without God they were "not right for the part." Realizing this, they surrendered (there's that word again) their lives to Jesus Christ and asked God to "take control" of their lives, rather than trying to rule themselves. Because of this decision they were given, by God, supernatural power for living.

Several years ago a man wrote a book in which he said the most important thing on earth is "Looking out for Number One." On the dedication page of the book he wrote: "Dedicated to the hope that somewhere in our universe there exists a civilization where the inhabitants possess sole dominion over their own lives."

There is such a place. It's called Hell. It is the place where men have totally divorced themselves from God's claim on their lives.

But the truly successful person has learned that in order to have power for living—supernatural power for living—he must be properly related to God.

Psychologists tell us there are, built into each of us, five basic needs. These are needs for:

POWER
◆ FOR
LIVING...
THE FIRST STEP

In closing, let me remind you that the Bible says, "I write these things to you who believe in the name of the Son of God so that you may *know* that you have eternal life" (I John 5:13).

Arthur S. DeMoss
(1925–1979)

Printed in USA
Bible quotations from the *New International Version*
American Tract Society • P.O. Box 462008 • Garland, Texas 75046

1. Security
2. Recognition
3. Love
4. Adventure
5. The need to create.

These are sometimes called "drives." These drives, either individually, or through a combination, control our lives. They are neither good nor evil. They are simply part of human nature. But it is these drives which cause us to walk out on a log in the forest and speak to the stream, telling it the deep things of our heart. It is these drives which, in the end, either push us into the arms of a loving Heavenly Father or, because we seek their fulfillment in some selfish or perverted way, drive us into hell.

If you don't find your answers to these drives in God, your human nature will force you to find them elsewhere— apart from God. It is when these drives are not met in God that you begin to feel inadequate—defeated. You feel like Charlie Brown: "Not right for the part."

It will always be this way until you enter the Kingdom of God. But once you've entered that Kingdom through a personal relationship with God, you are right for the part. From that time on you can say with confidence: "I am numbered among those who have been called by God. I have been chosen. I have a place in history."

Surely this is one of the things to be "born again" must mean. It means we're special to God.

Several years ago Fred Craddock was lecturing at Yale University. He told of going back one summer to Gatlin-burg, Tennessee, to take a short vacation with his wife. One night they found a quiet little restaurant where they looked forward to a private meal—just the two of them.

While they were waiting for their meal they noticed a distinguished looking, white-haired man moving from table to table, visiting guests. Craddock whispered to his wife, "I hope he doesn't come over here." He didn't want the man to intrude on their privacy.

But the man did come by his table.

"Where you folks from?" he asked amicably.

"Oklahoma."

"Splendid state, I hear, although I've never been there. What do you do for a living?"

"I teach homiletics at the graduate seminary of Phillips University."

"Oh, so you teach preachers, do you. Well, I've got a story I want to tell you." And with that he pulled up a chair and sat down at the table with Craddock and his wife.

Dr. Craddock said he groaned inwardly. Oh no, here comes another preacher story. It seems everyone has one.

The man stuck out his hand. "I'm Ben Hooper. I was born not far from here across the mountains. My mother wasn't married when I was born so I had a hard time. When I started to school my classmates had a name for me, and it wasn't a very nice name. I used to go off by myself at recess and during lunchtime because of the taunts of my playmates cut so deeply.

"What was worse was going downtown on Saturday afternoon and feeling every eye burning a hole through you. They were all wondering just who my real father was.

"When I was about 12 years old a new preacher came to our church. I would always go in late and slip out early.

But one day the preacher said the benediction so fast I got caught and had to walk out with the crowd. I could feel every eye in church on me. Just about the time I got to the door I felt a big hand on my shoulder. I looked up and the preacher was looking right at me.

" 'Who are you, son? Whose boy are you?'

"I felt the old weight come on me. It was like a big, black cloud. Even the preacher was putting me down.

"But as he looked down at me, studying my face, he began to smile a big smile of recognition. 'Wait a minute,' he said, 'I know who you are. I see the family resemblance. You are a son of God.'

"With that he slapped me across the rump and said, 'Boy, you've got a great inheritance. Go and claim it.' "

The old man looked across the table at Fred Craddock and said, "That was the most important single sentence ever said to me." With that he smiled, shook the hands of Craddock and his wife, and moved on to another table to greet old friends.

Suddenly, Fred Craddock remembered. On two occasions the people of Tennessee had elected an illegitimate to be their governor. His name was Ben Hooper.

That's what it means to be chosen by God. Although we have been born in iniquity, and although we have chosen to go our own way, through the blood of Jesus Christ we are saved—not only from our past, but from the fear of failure in our present and from powerless living in our future as well.

We have a great inheritance. The power for living that comes to us from God will enable us to go and claim it.

If you declare with your lips, "Jesus is
Lord," and believe in your heart that God
raised him from the dead, you will be
saved. For we believe in our hearts and
are put right with God; we declare with
our lips and are saved.

Romans 10:9,10 *(The Living Bible)*

HOW TO GET RIGHT WITH GOD

In the last chapter I pointed out that you are special to God. In fact, you are so special, God sent His Son, Jesus Christ, so you can have power for living. This cost Jesus His life, but by His death—and His resurrection from the dead—you can not only be forgiven and have eternal life, but you can have the power to overcome fear and live abundantly here on earth.

As a child I had two great fears. One was the fear of being left alone. The other was the fear of the unknown.

I was always afraid my father and mother would die and leave me alone. I was afraid I would have to go live with my uncle and aunt in Indiana. These fears haunted me day and night.

I remember the night I was left home with my mother while my father was out of town. My mother was sick, and when I tried to help her get out of bed to go to the bathroom, she fainted on the floor. She was too heavy for me to move. I had the presence of mind to call our family doctor, who was an old friend and lived not too far from our rural house. He came over, got my mother back into her bed, and told me not to be afraid.

But I was afraid. I stayed awake all night, my nose pressed against the screen in the window, wishing my father would pull up in the driveway so I wouldn't have to be alone.

I was also terrified by the fear of the unknown. Occasionally our family would drive north from our home in Florida to visit my mother's relatives in Kentucky, or to pay a visit to my father's sister in Indiana. I dreaded those trips because we always spent the night in tourist homes on the road. Those were the days before motels were popular. Instead, travelers stayed in what were called tourist homes or rooming houses in the small towns on the way. These were usually big, old houses which an old couple, or perhaps a widow, would open up to take in overnight lodgers.

I dreaded staying in these strange homes. Invariably I would have to stay in a room at the end of the hall on the third floor. If I was fortunate I got to sleep in the same bed with my younger brother. The beds were usually creaky, old, iron poster beds with exposed metal springs. The walls would be covered with the pictures of people who no doubt had lived and died in that same room. All through the night I would waken and see them staring down at me from their dusty picture frames.

Equally frightening was rain at night. It was always a terrifying situation to drive into a strange city at night with the rain peppering against the windshield. I would huddle close to my daddy and wish I were back in the familiar surroundings of my home in Florida.

That all came back to me last winter when I went on a hunting trip with some of my friends deep in the Florida Everglades. One of the men in the group owned a small cabin perched in a clump of live oaks and cabbage palms called a "hammock." This was surrounded on all sides by low, marshy ground. As far as the eye could see there was swamp, dotted with these "hammocks"—all of which looked alike.

The first afternoon we were there one of the men took us out into the swamp in a Jeep with oversized tires. He let each man off at a separate deer stand, about a mile apart and approximately two miles from the cabin. He promised to come back before dark to pick us up.

Shortly before dark it began to rain—a soft, misting rain. I pulled my rifle under my pancho and snuggled against the trunk of the huge oak tree where I was perched on a limb, high off the ground. It began to get dark, and I could hear the rain drops dripping loudly on the palm fronds below me. I began to think, "What am I doing up here in this tree in the middle of the Everglades when I could be home in my nice warm bed instead? Besides, I don't even like to kill things. The only reason I'm here is to be with my son, Tim, who is getting ready to leave for college. And I'm not even with him because he's on a deer stand on the other side of the swamp."

I slipped down out of the tree and started back to the cabin. The rain was falling harder now, and darkness had totally enveloped the swamp. I made my way through the thick hammock where I had been sitting and across an open glade. I was sloshing through ankle deep water in tall grass

looking for the barbed wire fence which marked the edge of
the section where we were hunting.

By now it was completely dark. I found the fence where
my friend was supposed to pick me up, but there was no sign
of a truck. Perhaps he had already come by and, thinking I
had walked back to the cabin, gone on. I had no choice but to
try to find my way back to the cabin in the dark.

Finding some higher ground along the fence line, I
slogged on through the misting rain, following the fence to
a gate. I knew at that point I had to turn left across an open
glade and walk about a mile. But there were no landmarks.
No stars. Only the dark, shadowy silhouettes of the various
hammocks against the darkening horizon. I searched the
ground, found the impressions of the truck tires, and set off
across the glade in a hopeless quest of following the tire
tracks in the dark. I knew the cabin was located in one of
those dark clumps of trees but had no idea which one. I was
literally feeling my way when it occurred to me I was lost.
Unless someone came out looking for me, I just might have
to spend the night in the swamp.

I waited for the old feelings of fear to set in, the
gnawing in the pit of my stomach, the sting of tears in my
eyes—all the old sensations I used to have as a child when I
was left alone or was in a strange place. But there was
nothing. No fear. No anxiety. Just a simple resignation that
if I had to spend the night in the swamp I'd better try and
find a dry spot.

I stumbled upon a small cattle feeder, a little shed-like
structure which protected a block of salt for the range cows
that wandered free in this section of the swamp. But as I

knelt down to see if it was dry under the little roof, I spotted, far in the distance, a light shining through the trees in one of the hammocks. It was our cabin. In a short while I was safe in the warm, dry house preparing for a dinner of smoked turkey with my friends—all of whom (including my son) thought it was a great joke that I had been lost in the dark.

That night, lying on my cot, listening in the darkness to the rain drizzling on the tin roof of the cabin, I reflected on my feelings. What had happened to the old fear? Where was the old gut-wrenching terror of the past? It wasn't until the next morning that I fully realized what had happened to me.

I was back on the deer stand at dawn. Only this time I didn't climb up in my tree. I leaned my unloaded rifle on a log and stood at the edge of the woods, watching the sun come up, listening as the world came alive at dawn. Moments before it had been totally silent. Not a sound, not a leaf moving. Then, as the eastern sky began to turn first light blue, then a soft rose color, a bird chirped. Then a squirrel moved. I heard the rustle of a racoon family coming through the tall grass. An armadillo scurried in front of me, his long nose probing the ground for grubs and beetles. Butterflies and mosquito hawks sailed gracefully overhead. Next came the sound of many birds chirping, squirrels barked in the trees and scampered along the low branches of the big oaks. And in the distance I heard the gobbling of a flock of wild turkeys.

Then, on the far side of the small glade where I was standing, I spotted him—a magnificent buck. He was stand-

So do not fear, for I am with you; do not
be dismayed, for I am your God. I will
strengthen you and help you; I will
uphold you with my righteous right hand.

Isaiah 41:10

ing head erect, his rack of horns crowning his regal head. He sniffed the air, looked directly at me, and slowly turned and entered the woods. He and I were part of the same creation—citizens of this marvelous garden of nature.

I stood for long moments, scarcely breathing, my heart beating in tune with all the sounds around me. The rain the night before had sweetened the air and freshened the earth. The golden sun rose in the east behind the clumps of cabbage palms, and suddenly the entire earth was alive with color and sound. I heard myself singing an old hymn:

> When morning gilds the skies
> My heart awakening cries,
> May Jesus Christ be praised.
>
> The night becomes as day,
> When from the heart we say,
> May Jesus Christ be praised.
>
> The powers of darkness fear
> When this sweet chant they hear:
> May Jesus Christ be praised.

That's it. The powers of darkness no longer had dominion over me. Why? Because a number of years before I had given my life to Jesus Christ. That which used to terrify me no longer controlled me. Now, through Jesus, I had power for living. I had appropriated what the apostle Paul had told his young friend, Timothy: *"For God hath not given us a spirit of fear, but of power, of love and of a sound mind"* (II Timothy 1:7 KJV).

How does one give his life to Jesus Christ? How can you come into this intimate fellowship with the Lord God of the universe who takes away our fear and replaces it with power?

Just as there are physical laws that govern the physical universe—causing the rain to fall and the sun to rise—so there are spiritual laws which govern your relationship with God. Submitting to these laws will allow Jesus Christ to become the Lord of your life. When that happens, He replaces your old power with His supernatural power for living.

LAW ONE:

God loves you and offers a wonderful plan for your life.

GOD'S LOVE
"For God so loved the world, that He gave His only begotten Son, that whoever believes in Him should not perish, but have eternal life" (John 3:16)

GOD'S PLAN
"I came that they might have life, and might have it abundantly" (John 10:10).

But as we've already seen, simply knowing that God loves you and has a wonderful plan for your life isn't enough. There are things which block us from God's love. And that brings us to the next law.

LAW TWO:

Man is sinful and separated from God.

Because of this he cannot know and experience God's love and God's plan for his life.

MAN IS SINFUL
"For all have sinned and fall short of the glory of God." (Romans 3:23).

You see, man was created to have fellowship with God. Just as I was able to stand in the Everglades and feel God's presence all around me without fear, so God wants you to have fellowship with Him. It is the same kind of fellowship Adam and Eve had with God in the Garden of Eden before sin entered the world. There, these two friends of God walked with Him in the cool of the evening, talking with their Creator as a son and daughter talk to their daddy.

But then Adam and Eve decided to go their own way rather than God's way. They broke fellowship with God, and ever since then man has chosen to go his own independent way. Sometimes this self-will is exercised in active rebellion against God. Sometimes it is expressed in passive indifference toward God. In whatever form it appears, this self-will is what the Bible calls *sin.*

MAN IS SEPARATED

"For the wages of sin is death" (spiritual separation from God) (Romans 6:23).

This diagram illustrates that God is holy and man is sinful. A great gulf separates the two. The arrows illustrate that man continually tries to reach God and the abundant life through his own efforts, such as living a good life, philosophy or even religion. The third law explains the only way we can bridge this gulf.

LAW THREE:

Jesus Christ is God's only provision for man's sin.

Through Him you can know and experience God's love and God's plan for your life.

HE DIED IN OUR PLACE

"But God demonstrates His own love toward us, in that while we were yet sinners, Christ died for us" (Romans 5:8).

HE ROSE FROM THE DEAD

"Christ died for our sins . . . He was buried . . . He was raised on the third day, according to the Scriptures . . . He appeared to Peter, then to the twelve. After that He appeared to more than five hundred . . ." (I Cor. 15:3-6).

HE IS THE ONLY WAY TO GOD

"Jesus said to him, 'I am the way, and the truth, and the life; no one comes to the Father, but through me' " (John 14:6).

This diagram illustrates that God has bridged the gulf which separates us from Him by sending His Son, Jesus Christ, to die on the cross in our place—to pay the penalty for our sins. But it is not enough to know these three laws. We also need to know the fourth one.

LAW FOUR:

We must individually receive Jesus Christ as Saviour
and Lord.

Then we can know and experience God's love and
plan for our lives.

WE MUST RECEIVE CHRIST
*"But as many as received Him, to them He gave the
right to become children of God, even to those who
believe in His name"* (John 1:12).

WE MUST RECEIVE CHRIST THROUGH FAITH
*"For by grace you have been saved through faith; and
that not of yourselves, it is the gift of God; not as a
result of works, that no one should boast"* (Ephesians 2:8,9).

WHEN WE RECEIVE CHRIST WE EXPERIENCE NEW BIRTH.
*"Jesus declared, 'I tell you the truth, unless a man is
born again, he cannot see the Kingdom of God' "* (John 3:3).

WE RECEIVE CHRIST BY PERSONAL INVITATION.
*"Behold, I stand at the door and knock; if any one
hears my voice and opens the door, I will come in to
him"* (Revelation 3:10).

Receiving Christ means we have to turn to Him. In order to do this we have to turn away from our sin. We cannot do this in our own power. But we must be willing to relinquish our sin and to surrender to Him all the rights to our life. Then, in an act of faith, we invite Jesus Christ to take over the control of our life. While that may seem difficult, it is in reality a very simple thing. All you do is, by an act of your will, say, "I want You, Jesus, to take over my life."

If you mean it with all your heart—He will.

Let me illustrate it by these two circles which represent two kinds of lives: the self-directed life and the Christ-directed life:

SELF-DIRECTED LIFE

S — Self is on the throne
+ — Christ is outside
● — interests are directed by self, often resulting in discord and frustration

CHRIST-DIRECTED LIFE

+ — Christ is in the life and on the throne
S — Self is yielding to Christ
● — interests are directed by Christ, resulting in harmony with God's plan

Which circle best represents your life?

Which circle would you like to have represent your life?

HOW YOU CAN RECEIVE JESUS CHRIST

When you stop and realize you were created by God for one purpose—so you could have fellowship with Him— then it stands to reason that God's greatest purpose for you is to have that fellowship restored. How is this done? It happens when you accept God's Son, Jesus Christ, as your Lord—the one who will—from this time on—direct your life.

"Well," you ask, "does that mean I have to join a church?

What about the bad habits in my life? Don't I have to give them up before I'm worthy to have fellowship with God?

"I've done too many bad things. I don't believe God will take me the way I am. Don't I have to do something first before He'll receive me?"

Let's put these questions aside for a while, because right now they don't make any difference. All of them are based on the presupposition you have to *do* something before God will receive you. But remember the scripture verse we looked at a moment ago from Ephesians? It pointed out that our relationship with God is not by "works," but it is a "gift of God." None of us could ever earn or deserve God's love and forgiveness. But He makes it freely available to anyone who will stop trusting in his own good works and efforts and will place all his faith in Jesus Christ to save him.

The wonderful thing is that you don't have to wait for God to receive you. He is waiting for you to receive Him.

Here's how you do it. You simply get alone somewhere and tell God that you believe in Him, that you cannot go on living without Him, that you are now accepting Jesus Christ as your Lord, and that from this time on you are going to allow Jesus to sit on the throne of your life.

Here's a simple prayer you can pray. In fact, if after reading this prayer it voices how you feel, you can read it over again and make it *your* prayer. When you do that God will hear you—and Jesus will come into your life as Lord.

"Dear God, I've been living my life my own way. Now I want to live it your way. I need you and I am now willing for you to take control of my life. I receive your son Jesus Christ, as my personal Saviour and Lord. I believe He died for my sins and has risen from the dead. I surrender to Him as Lord. Come, Lord Jesus, and occupy the throne of my life. Make me the kind of person you want me to be."

That's all there is to it. Oh, there's much more to come, and that's what the rest of this book is all about. But right here is where it all begins. And now that you've accepted Christ, and have allowed Him to move onto the throne of your life, you should *expect* some tremendous changes to take place. We'll be talking about those changes, too, and what you can expect.

You see, as a new citizen of the Kingdom of God, you have certain rights and privileges you've never had before. These are exciting things, for Christianity is not just a matter of *surrendering,* it is also a matter of receiving the

marvelous gifts Jesus brings with Him when He takes
control of your life. In fact, the moment that you, as an act of
faith, received Christ, many things happened, including the
following:

FIRST, Christ came into your life. Have you seen one
of those little toy cars in the department store? It looks real
enough, but if you examine the box it came in you'll see a
little notice: "Batteries not included." Without batteries—
no matter how authentic it looks—it won't run. You are
made in the image of God but because of sin your batteries
never did work. When Christ came into your life He
brought His power with Him.

Look at the words of Jesus. *"Here I am! I stand at the
door and knock. If anyone hears my voice and opens the
door, I will go in and eat with him, and he with me"* (Revelation
3:20). Paul says it this way: *"Christ in you, the hope of glory"*
(Colossians 1:27). That's exciting. And powerful.

SECOND, your sins were forgiven. When my oldest
daughter was about two years old she climbed up on my
dresser and found a ring which had been given me by my
father. It was not a valuable ring, but it had a lot of senti-
mental meaning to me. Robin played with it for a while,
then flushed it down the toilet. The next day, when I asked if
anyone had seen my ring, she admitted her sin. Even though
I punished her, I was unable to forgive her. The ring was
that meaningful to me.

The next afternoon I came in from work and settled in
my chair with the newspaper. When I looked up there stood
my four-year-old son. Beside him, with tears on her cheeks,

was little Robin. Bruce did the talking. "Robin's sorry she lost your ring, Daddy. But we made you a new one this afternoon."

He held out his hand. In it was a ring—braided out of pine needles.

I swept them both into my arms and held them close to my chest. Not once since that time have I missed my old ring, nor have I ever again blamed my daughter for what she did. Because of the action of her brother, she was forgiven. Totally.

That is what Jesus did for us. He went to the Father and paid the price of our sin. Because of Him, Paul says in Colossians 1:14, "we have redemption, the forgiveness of sins."

THIRD, you became a child of God. In fact, the Bible says, you now have the same rights as the Son of God, Jesus Christ. These are inherited rights because you are now an heir of God and a joint heir with Jesus Christ.

"To all who received Him...He gave the right to become children of God," one of Jesus' biographers tells us in John 1:12.

Something like this happened to my younger sister. After my parents had four sons they decided to adopt a little girl. She was only a few days old when my mother brought her home from the hospital. Although a woman other than his wife had given birth to her, my father fully accepted Audrey as his own child. She grew up as a Buckingham and has shared equally in everything belonging to the family.

Recently I was meeting with a group of men at a retreat lodge near where Audrey lives in Missouri. One afternoon she drove out to the retreat center to visit me. Although none of the men in the group had ever met her before—in fact, none of them even knew I had a sister—when she showed up at the retreat center looking for me several men recognized her as my sister.

Across the years we've even begun to look alike. She is my father's daughter—fully accepted into the family.

FOURTH, you received eternal life. That may not mean much to you right now, but in the long run it is the most important thing that can ever happen to you. Eternal life means you not only belong to the family of God, but because Jesus died and then rose from the dead, overcoming death, you, too, will live forever.

Death is man's greatest enemy. It is man's greatest fear. But as a child of God, you no longer have to fear death. The grave may hold your body, but *you* will live on forever with Jesus Christ in Heaven. *"And this is the testimony: God has given us eternal life, and this life is in his Son. He who has the Son has life; he who does not have the Son of God does not have life. I write these things to you who believe in the name of the Son of God so that you may know that you have eternal life"* (I John 5:11-13).

FINALLY, you began the great adventure for which God created you.

Jesus said, *"I have come that they may have life, and have it to the full"* (John 10:10). It's not just life after death which Jesus gives us. He also gives us full and abundant life here on earth. He gives us power for living—now!

"If anyone is in Christ," Paul tells us, *"he is a new creation; the old has gone, the new has come!"* (I Corinithians 5:17). All the adventure of the universe is yours to experience, all the joy of being on the winning side, all the wisdom of God, all the peace of Heaven—it is all yours... and more... because of Jesus.

Now, before we go on, let's pause and review those four laws that brought you into your new relationship with God. In fact, you might find it helpful to list these statements on cards and review them regularly—until you know them by heart. That way, when others start asking you what has brought about the marvelous changes they'll see in your life, you can share these same laws with them.

1. God loves you and offers a wonderful plan for your life.
2. Man is sinful and separated from God. Therefore, he cannot have fellowship with God or receive God's full love.
3. Jesus Christ is the only way man can approach God. Through Him, however, you can experience God's love and His plan for your life.
4. Each person must receive Christ individually. It is not enough to belong to a church or have Christian parents. But if you receive Him, He will make you a "son of God" also.

HOW TO KNOW THAT CHRIST IS IN YOUR LIFE

People often ask, "How can I know for sure that I am a Christian—that Christ has come into my life?" Remember the promise we looked at in Revelation 3:20? Here Jesus says, ***"If any man hear my voice and open the door, I will come in to him..."*** You can know on the authority of the trustworthiness of God Himself and His Word that Christ has come into your life.

Thank God often that Christ is in your life and that He will never leave you (Hebrews 13:5). You can know that the living Christ indwells you and that you have eternal life, from the moment you invite Him in on the basis of His promise. He will not deceive you.

Can you think of anything more wonderful that could happen to you than receiving Christ? Before reading any further, why don't you close this book and thank God in prayer for what He has done for you. Remember, your relationship with God is not based on your "feelings." You may not feel any different now than you did before you prayed the prayer accepting Christ. The feelings wil come later. Right now accept your salvation by faith. Christ is Lord of your life because God said—in His Bible—that if you receive Him, Jesus will take control.

LIVING BY FAITH

The problem is that most of us don't really trust God to do what He says He will do in the Bible. The Bible says *"the just shall live by faith"* and *"without faith it is impossible to please God."* The object of our faith, then, is God Himself. Once we understand who God is—that He is not only holy and righteous, but He is loving, forgiving, all-wise and full of mercy—we should have no problem trusting Him.

God, the Bible says, loves us unconditionally. In other words, no matter what you do behind God's back—or to His face—He loves you. Once we understand that, we can ask His forgiveness and then trust Him with our lives totally and completely.

Many people are afraid of God. They see Him as some kind of "super fuzz," a huge cop sitting behind a cloud with a spiritual radar gun waiting to catch them disobeying the law so He can punish them. As a result they are unwilling to totally surrender their life to Him for fear He'll slap them in leg irons and put them to work on the road gang. Better to stay as far away from God as possible, they feel.

Maybe you have felt this way about God. You felt if you gave your life to Jesus Christ that God would march you off to some concentration camp and beat the life out of you. Nothing is farther from the truth. Instead of putting us in prison, faith in Christ sets us free.

I like the illustration used by Bill Bright, founder of Campus Crusade for Christ. Dr. Bright says: "My wife and I have two grown sons. Suppose that when they were little boys they had come to greet me when I returned home from a trip and said, 'We love you. We missed you. We are so excited about your being home. We have been talking together and we have decided that we will do anything yo want us to do. From now on, you issue the command and we will obey without any questions. We just want to please you.'

"What do you think," Dr. Bright asks, "would have been my attitude in response to their expressions of love for me? If I had responded the way many people think God will respond if they said to Him, 'Lord, I'll do anything you want me to do. I'll go anywhere you want me to go,' I would have taken them by the shoulders, looked at them with an evil eye and said, 'I have just been waiting for you to say that. Now I'm going to make you regret your decision to trust as long as you live. I am going to take all the fun out of your lives. I will make you miserable as long as you live.'

"No, I wouldn't have said that. I would have put my arms around them and given them a big hug and said, 'Zac, Brad, I love you, too, and want to justify your faith in me. I want to be a better father to you. I want to do everything I can to help you find full and meaningful lives."

Do you think God would do anything less for you? Remember, He loves you with an everlasting love. He sent His only Son to die for you and pay the penalty of your sin. No, He wants to bless you. He wants to give you power for living. But He cannot bless you unless you trust and obey Him—unless you are willing to live by faith.

As you exercise faith in an unlimited God and draw upon His unlimited resources, you will begin to experience the abundant life which Jesus came to give!

Brothers, I do not consider myself yet to
have taken hold of it. But one thing I do:
Forgetting what is behind and straining
toward what is ahead, I press on toward
the goal to win the prize for which God
has called me heavenward in Christ Jesus.

Philippians 3:13,14

HOW TO
KEEP ON GROWING

Becoming a Christian is only the beginning of a wonderful new life. God rarely takes people to heaven the moment they become Christians. He has work for you to do here on earth.

Being "born again" is like hatching out of an egg. Long before your birth, even before your conception, God had *you* in mind. All along God has had a distinct purpose for you to fulfill on earth and in eternity. But you will never find or fulfill that wonderful purpose unless you grow as a Christian. Simply being hatched is not enough. You need to fly.

Soren Kierkegaard, the Danish philosopher, once told a story about a flock of barnyard geese in Denmark. Every Sunday the geese would gather in the barnyard near the feeding trough. One of their number, a "preaching goose," would struggle up on the top rail of the fence and exhort the geese about the glories of goosedom. He would tell them how wonderful it was to be a goose, rather than a chicken or a turkey. He would remind them of their great heritage and tell them of the marvelous possibilities in the future.

Occasionally, while he was preaching, a flock of wild geese, winging south from Sweden, across the Baltic Sea on their way to sunny France, would fly overhead in a marvelous V-formation—thousands of feet in the air. When that happened, all the geese would excitedly look and say to one another, "That's who we really are. We are not destined to spend our lives in this stinking barnyard. Our destiny is to fly."

But then the wild geese would disappear from sight, their honkings echoing across the horizon. The barnyard geese would look around at their comfortable surroundings, sigh, and return to the mud and filth of the barn.

They never did fly.

Sadly, there are a number of people in the Kingdom of God who remain in the barnyard, rather than spread their wings and learn to fly.

God has a purpose for YOU.

Salvation—in its highest sense—is the process of becoming who you really are in God's mind.

Conversion—being born again—is an event. It only happens once. It is the experience of moving from darkness to light, from death to life. Salvation, on the other hand, is a process. It begins at conversion and continues until you are fully transformed into the image of Jesus Christ.

MOVING ON FROM SPIRITUAL INFANCY

There are a number of things which keep us in the barnyard of infant Christianity, when God's highest purpose for us is to grow to flying maturity. It may be we're unwilling to run the risk of failure. Now that I'm a Christian, you might say, and I know I'm going to heaven, why do more?

Others are afraid to leave the comforts of the barnyard for the rugged life of faith. But anything worth having has its price. People who want to move on to spiritual maturity are willing to pay the price. These are the ones whom God uses in special ways to shape the world.

Paul told his friends at Philippi to *"continue to work out your salvation with fear and trembling, for it is God who works in you to will and to act according to his good purpose"* (Philippians 2:13).

He was not talking about entering the Kingdom of God by good works. Remember, we read earlier that you do not work your way into the good graces of God. No, he was talking about the "process" of salvation whereby you grow in grace and are conformed to the image of God's Son, Jesus Christ. He was saying that growth as a Christian demands cooperation with God. In fact, he said you had to work at it. Then God, who works in you through His Holy Spirit, will make things happen.

In the next chapter Paul goes ahead and warns the church at Philippi against stopping along the way in their Christian life. He told them there was "more"—more than they had yet experienced in Christ. He was, in essence, telling them to grow as Christians.

"One thing I do: forgetting what is behind and straining toward what is ahead, I press on toward the goal to win the prize for which God has called me heavenward in Christ Jesus" (Philippians 3:13-14).

Paul constantly warned his friends of the danger of not growing. In fact, he went so far as to say he feared becoming "spiritually shipwrecked" if he failed to grow. *"Do you not know that in a race all the runners run, but only one gets the prize? Run in such a way as to get the prize ... I do not run like a man running aimlessly; I do not fight like a man beating the air. No, I beat my body and make it my slave so that after I have preached to others, I myself will not be disqualified for the prize"* (I Corinthians 9:24-27).

It sounds like Paul took this Christian life pretty seriously. He knew if he did not grow as a Christian, if he did not move forward, he could easily fall back into the old life. If this was such a major concern to a man like Paul, it seems the rest of us ought to take growth seriously as well.

The saddest of all people are those Christians who do not go on to full growth, who never leave the spiritual "nursery," who remain in diapers and booties rather than donning the gear of the mountain climber in order to scale the heights with the help of the Holy Spirit.

TOOLS TO ACCOMPLISH THE TASK

One of the purposes of this book is to give you the proper tools necessary to climb those magnificent mountains to spiritual maturity. Maybe a good way to understand these tools is by looking at the word "Growth" in this acrostic:

G Go to God in prayer daily (John 15:7).
R Read God's Word daily (Acts 17:11).
O Obey God, moment by moment (John 14:21).
W Witness for Christ by your life and words (Matthew 4:19).
T Trust God for every detail of your life (I Peter 5:7).
H Holy Spirit—Allow God to control and empower your daily life (Galatians 5:16,17; Acts 1:8).

G

GO TO GOD IN PRAYER DAILY

Prayer is simply talking to God—and listening while God talks. It is the most basic expression of our faith. It is the "breathing" of our spiritual life. It is our lifeline to God.

Many people mistakenly think prayer needs to be formal—with "thees and thous." Not so. Prayer is nothing more than a child talking to his Daddy. It can be:

A cry for help in a time of need.
A squeal of delight for receiving a gift.
A plea in behalf of someone else.

A quiet time of adoration.
A period of listening as God talks.
A gentle time of receiving God's love.
Prayer is basically conversation with our Heavenly Father.

"Forgive me, Father. I really blew it this time. I didn't want to explode at my son, but I did it anyway. Will you now give me strength to ask *his* forgiveness also?"

"Lord, remember last year when I began asking you for money to buy this new car. My faith wasn't very strong back then, was it? But oh, how I thank you for your faithfulness. You provided. Now the car is ours. Thank you, thank you."

"Help me, God. I've been over this checkbook a dozen times and it still won't balance. Please show me where I made my mistake."

"O God, I'm not worthy to even talk to you. I've messed up my body with all these drugs, I've destroyed my loved ones...O God...I need help. Please help me."

"Well, Lord, I've just signed the biggest contract of my life. Now I've got to produce. All I have is yours, I'm just asking you to take over my brain so I can get the job done."

"Father, I've been battling this problem long enough. Now I'm going to turn it over to you and ask you to treat me as a little child until I learn my lesson."

Do you know any energetic, joyful Christians? You know, the kind that smile all the time, who seem to love everyone, who are on top of their problems. Almost certainly, they know a secret: *prayer provides power for living.*

HOW DOES GOD ANSWER PRAYER?

Remember, God wants to grant your requests much more than the most loving father on earth wishes to give his children good things. But remember, too, He is your Father. As any good father, He knows how to give good gifts—and when to give them.

This means sometimes God says "No" to our requests. However, He never says "No" without having a better answer waiting for us just around the bend of the road.

It's important to remember this: When God says "No" to us, it's *not* because He can't afford it. Nor is it because He doesn't care. God is the owner of everything—riches, knowledge, wisdom, power, health, joy and love. Not only that, but He cares for us. He loves us more than any earthly father could ever love us. Thus, even though God does—on occasion—say "No," this is the exception. His usual response to us is "Yes!"

That's the reason, when we pray, we should *expect* a "Yes" answer.

When we know from the Bible what God's will is in a matter, and act on that will even though we have yet to see it taking place in our lives, we open the door for God to answer our prayers even more quickly.

WRITE DOWN YOUR ANSWERS

I recommend you keep a prayer notebook. I have such a journal. It is just a little looseleaf notebook where I keep my prayer requests. On one page I write down my request. On the opposite page I note when and how God answered that request. As I look back over my notebook I am amazed to discover that about 97% of my prayers of five years ago have been answered—and the rest are being answered.

I don't pray for everything every day. Some things I pray for only once a week—on specific days. But I keep my prayer journal just as faithfully as I brush my teeth. And I pray just as faithfully.

Writing down God's answers has encouraged me and given me more faith. Every year I pray for bigger and more "impossible" things. Each year God keeps increasing my faith—and my "bigger" prayers now are answered just as easily as my smaller prayers were answered a number of years ago. This is one of the joys of growth. You get to measure your own progress—especially in your prayer life.

What's the most important thing to remember about prayer? Just this. Jesus said, *"I am the way and the truth and the life. No one comes to the Father except through me"* (John 14:6). This means for prayer to be real prayer, it should be in the name of Jesus. When you come to God in the name of His son, He pays attention.

R

READ GOD'S WORD DAILY

If prayer is your lifeline to God, then the Bible is the breadbasket. Just as it is important for you to develop good eating habits—eating regular meals of proper food—so it is

Your word is a lamp to my feet and a
light for my path.

Psalms 119:105

vitally important for you to feast at God's table, the Bible, every day.

Bible reading, like prayer, can be made into a habit. A good habit. The Bible is absolutely central to our lives. There are several reasons for this.

First, the Bible, by the power of God's Spirit, produces faith in our hearts. Remember, we said salvation was a process of growth. One of the ways you can achieve your growth potential is through daily Bible reading. If you don't eat, your body won't grow. Likewise, if you don't read your Bible, you'll never grow beyond spiritual infancy.

Secondly, the Bible continues to nourish us throughout our lives. Jesus prayed that the Bible would have this effect upon His followers: ***"Sanctify them by the truth; your word is truth"*** (John 17:17).

Sanctify means to "set apart" or "make holy." How does God make us holy? By bringing us into regular contact with His Word. As we "eat" His Word, as we "digest" it, it goes into all our spiritual cells, and we become filled with the Word of God.

Third, the Bible is our standard for making decisions and forming opinions in every area of life. ***"All Scripture is God-breathed and is useful for teaching, rebuking, correcting and training in righteousness, so that the man of God may be thoroughly equipped for every good work"*** (II Tim. 3:16,17).

Someone said the definition of a Christian was one whose life was totally dominated and controlled by the Lord Jesus Christ. How do you know what Jesus wants of you? By reading His Word. In the pages of the Bible you will find God's will for your life.

I often drive from my home in Melbourne, on the east coast of Florida, to the central Florida city of Orlando—about 70 miles away—for editorial meetings with the staff of the magazine where I work as editor-at-large. We have an excellent Christian radio station in Melbourne, and I enjoy listening to music on my car radio. However, as I drive away from Melbourne I begin to lose the station on my radio. I can do a certain amount of fine tuning, but eventually the station disappears, and almost at once I pick up an Orlando station which plays music I don't care for. The station back in Melbourne is still broadcasting. My radio is still working. The trouble is I have moved too far away to get clear reception.

When I drive back home from Orlando at the close of the day there is a spot along the highway where suddenly the Melbourne station is picked up. I'm back in range.

The reason I read my Bible daily is to keep me in range of God's voice. I make enough mistakes as it is without tuning out the Word of God from my life. A daily look at God's Word will give you access to God's wisdom and knowledge, keeping you safe from wrong decisions and filling you with power for living.

O

OBEY GOD,
MOMENT BY MOMENT

How can you know if you really love Jesus—that it's not some kind of phony or artificial love? One of the most exciting things in the world is that God has given us a *standard* for love. Here it is.

"Whosoever has my commands and obeys them, he is the one who loves me. He who loves me will be loved by my Father, and I too will love him and show myself to him" (John 14:21).

How do we know we love Jesus? Because we obey His commands. Of course, we don't have to "prove" anything to anybody. But obedience becomes the gauge by which we can check ourselves. *"And this is love: that we walk in obedience to his commands"* (II John 6).

If you love God, the Bible says, you will also love others. *"He has given us this command: Whoever loves God must also love his brother"* (I John 4:21). That's pretty plain.

ARE YOU "IN CHRIST"?

The term "in Christ" is used 165 times in the New Testament. In fact, in the first chapter of Ephesians it is used nine times. That means being "in Christ" must be important. What does it mean?

You are IN CHRIST when you obey the still small voice of the Holy Spirit as He interprets the Bible. The Holy

Therefore, as God's chosen people, holy
and dearly loved, clothe yourselves with
compassion, kindness, humility,
gentleness and patience. Bear with each
other and forgive whatever grievances
you may have against one another.
Forgive as the Lord forgave you.

Colossians 3:12,13

Spirit often speaks in a corrective voice. He is like those small rockets on the base of the giant rockets which carry the satellites into orbit. When the main rocket begins to veer off course, a command can be given from Mission Control which fires one of the small, directional rockets. This pushes the spaceship back on course. The Holy Spirit often speaks to us like this. We sometimes call it our "conscience," but for the Christian that is the voice of the Holy Spirit.

God does not bless disobedience. He may protect us while we are disobedient, but His blessings are reserved for those who obey Him. When we drive down the highway my wife sometimes reminds me that the minute I exceed the speed limit I am "on my own" as far as God's blessings are concerned. He may protect me if I drive in disobedience to the law, but I have literally driven out from under His blessing—for God wants us to obey those civil laws which are not in direct conflict with the Bible.

Living a life of obedience to God—moment by moment—insures your growth as a Christian.

Likewise, we are told to love our brothers and sisters. Paul described this family as a "body." He pointed out the body has many parts: hands, feet, knees, elbows, ears, plus a lot of parts we can't see—things like liver, spleen and heart. Each one of us serves as part of that body. Just because you are a finger should not make you upset because someone else is an eye. You are both important, even though you have different functions to perform.

If the eye has picked up a grain of sand, it needs the finger to help it out. An elbow or a foot simply won't get the job done. Likewise, the finger needs the eye so it can "see" where the cotton swab is which will take the grain of sand out of the eye. And both need the feet to take them into the bathroom to find the cotton swab. Then, have you ever tried to put your finger to your eye with a stiff elbow? All parts are necessary to the body.

Loving one another means we are one body. That body is called the church. It is not a building, it is not even an organization. It is a group of people—all different—who love the Lord and love each other. You need to be part of such a family if you are going to be obedient to God.

As you grow in your Christian life, remember the simple, yet profound, words of Jesus: *"If you love me, you will obey what I command"* (John 14:17).

W

WITNESS FOR CHRIST BY YOUR LIFE AND YOUR WORDS

Witnessing for Christ is simply being who you are. It does not mean that you need to preach, it doesn't necessarily mean you have to go door-to-door telling strangers about Jesus. All it means is living for Jesus every day so that not only your words tell of Christ, but your life reflects His life as well.

How do you witness with your life? By doing what we've just been discussing: obeying God's Word, being directed and controlled by the Holy Spirit, displaying the fruit of the Spirit in your actions and behavior.

This doesn't mean you have to become a prude, wear strange clothes, and be unable to have a good time. It doesn't even mean you have to carry your Bible around all day either. It simply means you stay attached to Jesus at all times.

Jesus described it as branches attached to a vine. He is the vine. We are the branches. If we stay attached, we will bear fruit and our lives will be a testimony to all around us.

A Christian nurse in a psychiatric clinic had several opportunities to speak of her faith to doctors in the clinic. They all thought she was a little strange but didn't object too much since she was an excellent employee.

Then that woman's much-beloved teenage son was killed in a motorcycle accident. In the weeks that followed, one physician after another came to the nurse privately, admiring her faith and questioning her about the inner strength she showed. Her calm demeanor and peaceful spirit in the face of deep grief "preached a silent sermon" each finally was able to hear.

As a witness for Jesus you will affect the entire world. *"You are the light of the world,"* Jesus told His followers. *"A city on a hill cannot be hidden. Neither do people light a lamp and put it under a bowl. Instead they put it on its stand, and it gives light to everyone in the house. In the same way, let your light shine before men, that they may see your good deeds and praise your Father in heaven"* (Matthew 5:14-16).

However, just being a witness with your life is not enough. Christian growth means you will also witness with your mouth. The redeemed of the Lord will "say so," says the Psalmist. That means once you've been saved and filled with His Holy Spirit, you're going to want to tell others about this wonderful way of life. It will come as naturally as telling others about the person you love. Or about your new car. Or about your child or grandchild. God will give you just the right words—and will provide just the right people to talk to. All you have to do is make yourself available.

T

TRUST GOD FOR EVERY DETAIL OF YOUR LIFE

When God placed you into His family, He took responsibility for your life and your problems. David said it better than anyone has ever said it: *"The Lord is my shepherd, I shall lack nothing"* (Psalm 23:1).

God is a God of unlimited resources. When you trust Him, you move beyond your understanding, beyond your comprehension, to a dimension of belief where you are willing to relax in life because you know there is a great, all-powerful, loving God watching over you. What, therefore, is there to fear?

How is this done?

When you reach the place that everything you own belongs to God, then everything God owns belongs to you.

It's that simple.

There are those who want to know God's will in advance so they may determine whether to do it or not. But

Life is more than food, and the body
more than clothes....Consider how the
lilies grow. They do not labor or spin.
Yet I tell you, not even Solomon in all
his splendor was dressed like one of
these. If that is how God clothes the
grass of the field, which is here today,
and tomorrow is thrown into the fire,
how much more will he clothe you, O
you of little faith!

Luke 12:23,27,28

God reveals His will only to those who are committed to follow it—"come what may."

Man's intellect is always trying to figure things out. He wants answers to all his "what if?" questions. God does not answer such questions, however. He simply says, "Trust me." That means God always reserves His best for those who leave the choices to Him. *"Commit your way unto the Lord, trust also in Him and He will bring it to pass"* (Psalm 37:5).

H

HOLY SPIRIT—ALLOW GOD TO CONTROL AND EMPOWER YOUR DAILY LIFE

As a Christian every day can be an exciting adventure. But in order for that to happen you must be filled with the Holy Spirit. Far too many believers stop with the act of becoming a Christian and never move on to the victorious life of walking in the Spirit.

Dr. Bill Bright, the Founder and President of Campus Crusade for Christ, says: "If there were only one truth I could share with the Christian world, it would be 'how to be filled with the Holy Spirit,' for there is no single truth that is more important to the believer."

That is a powerful statement. And since it is true, you need to ask yourself: "How can I be filled with the Holy Spirit?"

But first, let's ask some other basic questions.

WHO IS THE HOLY SPIRIT?

Maybe it would be easier if I first told you who He is not. He is not an "it." Nor is He a ghost—some kind of shadowy vapor. (The word "ghost" in the King James Bible, by the way, is the ancient translation of the word better translated "spirit.") The Holy Spirit is not some weird, ethereal, mystical feeling or impersonal presence.

The Holy Spirit is the third person of the Trinity: Father, Son and Holy Spirit. He is a real person. He has a personality. He has feelings. He may be hurt, grieved, loved, honored, known, and communicated with. He has infinite intellect, will, and emotion. He possesses all the divine nature of God. He is equal in every way with God, the Father and God the Son. And—this is most important—He is waiting to take control of your life.

WHY DID THE HOLY SPIRIT COME?

Before Jesus left earth, following His resurrection, He called his followers together and told them that when He returned to Heaven He would send the Holy Spirit back to earth. The Holy Spirit would actually live inside every believer! In fact, the same power that raised Christ from the dead could then control the life of every Christian.

The Spirit's ministry in a believer's life takes on many forms.

For one, He convicts us of our sin. Remember, He is a *Holy* Spirit. That means He is pure. When He fills us, He does so to purify us—to make us holy.

He also takes away our doubts—those pestering questions about our salvation. He convinces us we really are the Children of God—just as the Bible says.

The Holy Spirit makes the presence of Jesus real in us. When Jesus was on earth He spent a great deal of time with His disciples. He taught them and answered their questions. He was their most intimate friend. It's no wonder they grieved so deeply when He left them.

It was to them Jesus said, *"I will ask the Father, and he will give you another Counselor to be with you forever—the Spirit of truth"* (John 14:16-17). He arrived, just as Jesus promised, and has been with us ever since, making Jesus as real to every Christian as if He were still here in the flesh.

The Holy Spirit does many other things.

He teaches us.

He helps us when we don't know how to pray—actually praying through us. *"The Spirit helps us in our weakness. We do not know what we ought to pray, but the Spirit himself intercedes for us with groans that words cannot express"* (Romans 8:26).

He gives us power—supernatural power. In fact, Jesus told his disciples *"You will receive power when the Holy Spirit comes on you ... "* (Acts 1:8). Power for what? Well, for many things—but primarily to be witnesses of Jesus. Filled with the Holy Spirit, those disciples were transformed from a cowardly and defeated band of leaderless stragglers to a bold army of spiritual warriors who challenged, and defeated, the forces of hell which held the world in bondage.

But perhaps the most wonderful thing the Holy Spirit does is to produce in you the life of Jesus. When the Holy

Spirit is allowed to take control of your life, then Jesus, in all His character and personality, is at home in you. He will love and live through you. You will begin to see in your life what the Bible calls the "fruit of the Spirit": love, joy, peace, patience, kindness, goodness, faithfulness, gentleness, and self-control. It won't happen all at once, for no tree bears fruit overnight. But day by day you will see your life changing as you take on the character of Jesus. That's exciting.

WHAT DOES IT MEAN TO BE FILLED WITH THE HOLY SPIRIT?

At the very moment you were born again the Holy Spirit took up residence in your life. However, that does not mean you are "filled" with the Holy Spirit. To be filled means you are controlled and empowered. It means you are relying on the power of God to change your life, rather than trying to do it yourself. Power for living is yours only when you yield to Him and let Him control your life. You cannot live the Christian life in your own power through self-determination and self-discipline. Only Jesus was able to live a perfect life; and only as He lives in you—through His Spirit—can you live victoriously.

In a nutshell, to be filled with the Holy Spirit means to be filled with Jesus.

HOW CAN I BE FILLED
WITH THE HOLY SPIRIT?

Several years ago I visited one of those huge hydro-electric dams on the Columbia River in Washington state. I had heard of such things as turbines and generators, but for some reason had always thought the power from those dams was provided by the water which roared over the spillway. It never occured to me—a flatlander from Florida—that the real power was not in the froth which splattered over the top, but was produced in the hidden machines far below the top of the dam.

We took an elevator deep into the mysterious interior of the dam. Stepping out into a huge room, as long as the dam was wide, I was suddenly in the middle of more power than I had ever imagined possible. The spotless room, with the huge cranes overhead on their tracks, was filled with a deep "huummm." The very air was vibrating with power. Where did it come from? Not from the water which splashed over the spillway hundreds of feet above. Nor did it come from those giant, hidden turbines in the floor. It came from the millions of pounds of water pressure in the lake above. As the water moved through those slow turning turbines it created enough power to provide electricity for half the state of Washington and part of Oregon.

So does the Holy Spirit move through the spiritual turbine of the believer, creating incredible power.

Being filled with the Spirit involves a complete surrender of your will, without reservation, to the will of God. This is not an event—it is a process, a continual process.

Paul wrote to his friends in Ephesus and told them to be *"filled with the Spirit"* (Ephesians 5:18). His language means to be continually filled. What he is saying is, "be filled, and filled, and filled, and filled with the Holy Spirit."

Why do we need to keep on being filled with the Spirit? Well, for one thing, we often take back the control of our lives that we had already yielded to Him. We decide that we want to be our own master and make our own decisions. When we do, the Holy Spirit is grieved—that is, the flow of His power through us is hindered. In order to get this power restored we must agree with God that we have sinned, and once again yield the control of our lives to His Spirit.

Dr. Bill Bright refers to this experience as "spiritual breathing." While a baby takes its first breath shortly after it is born, unless it keeps on breathing it will die. Likewise Paul tells us to be filled *continually* with the Holy Spirit. Spiritual breathing means you exhale anything which hinders or "grieves" the Holy Spirit, and you continually inhale the power of the Holy Spirit. As you exhale impure air you then inhale pure air.

If you want to be filled with the Holy Spirit you need to exhale the impurities of sin in your life. This is known as confession—agreeing with God that you have sinned, that you have been in control of some area of your life and you are now exhaling that impurity. Then immediately thank God for forgiving your sin, and once again surrender the control of your life to Him.

You will want to make "spiritual breathing" a consistent part of your life, so that you can live each day filled with the wonderful power of the Holy Spirit.

It is possible that up until this moment, the Holy Spirit has been just a "guest" in your life. (Remember that He came to live in you the moment you became a Christian.) But He wants to be more than a guest. He wants to be the Master of your home. He wants complete access to the library of your mind, the dining room of your appetites, the parlor of your relationships, and the game room of your social life. He wants to be invited into the small, hidden rooms where you have previously engaged in shameful activity. In short, He wants to be in charge of your life.

That sounds like a pretty major surrender. And it is! But in exchange for surrendering your life to Him, the Holy Spirit fills you with supernatural power over sin, an abundant, meaningful life, and the indescribable love, joy, peace, patience, and goodness of Jesus Himself.

Like your salvation, the filling of the Holy Spirit is a gift of God. You cannot earn either. Both are received by faith and the complete yielding of your will to Him.

Do you want to be filled with the Holy Spirit? You don't have to search for Him—or wait for Him. He is already dwelling in you, waiting for you to allow Him to control your life. If this is the desire of your heart, then simply tell God that you want to be filled with the Holy Spirit, accept His power by faith, and begin to thank Him. All the power of Heaven is yours as you begin living the Spirit-filled life.

There you have it: GROWTH. Like children we are afraid to face it, but when it comes we think it's great. So your growth as a Christian will be both exciting—and useful.

By way of review we see that to move on from our initial conversion to spiritual maturity we need to use these special "tools."

G — Go to God in prayer daily
R — Read God's Word daily
O — Obey God moment by moment
W— Witness for Christ by your life and words
T — Trust God for every detail of your life
H — Holy Spirit: allow God to control and empower your daily life.

Your Christian growth gives glory to God and allows Him to bless you with His Presence—and that Presence brings power for living.

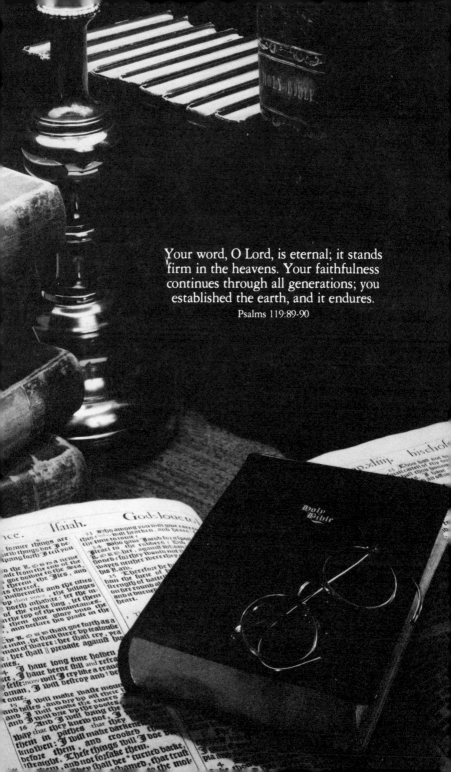

Your word, O Lord, is eternal; it stands firm in the heavens. Your faithfulness continues through all generations; you established the earth, and it endures.

Psalms 119:89-90

WHAT THE BIBLE IS ALL ABOUT

The Greek philosopher, Plato, once said there are three valid sources of knowledge.

1. The five senses—touch, taste, smell, sight, sound—which we share with the animal kingdom.

2. Reason—which sets man apart from the lower animals.

3. The third he called "Divine Madness"—by which he referred to the spiritual world of supernatural communication.

Later his disciple, Aristotle, eliminated the third source—the entire intuitive faculty by which divine perception comes to man. Aristotle said knowledge comes only through the five senses and reason.

Much of the western world was affected by what Aristotle taught. But in Eastern and primitive cultures reference to the spirit world—the world of dreams, visions and supernatural communication—is common in all walks of life.

While Aristotle would have rejected the Bible as a source of knowledge, Jesus never hesitated when He said the Bible is the primary way through which God reveals Himself to mankind.

Now, 2,000 years later, more and more people are seeing that Jesus was right. Voltaire, the famous French atheist (who was a follower of Aristotle rather than Jesus), died in 1778. Before dying he said the Bible and Christian faith would not be believed in one hundred years. On the 100th anniversary of his statement, the Geneva Bible Society purchased Voltaire's printing press and house and started to print Bibles from there.

Two hundred and six years after Voltaire, the President of the United States declared the year 1983 as "The Year of the Bible." Why would the president of the greatest nation in history proclaim the Bible as mankind's greatest source of knowledge?

Millions of people are looking for a reliable voice of authority. They have found they cannot trust treaties between nations, they cannot trust the statements of scientists; even the great religious leaders are often wrong. The Bible—the Word of God—is the only real authority we have. Proven across the years, the Bible sheds light on human nature, world problems and human suffering. But beyond that it clearly reveals *the way to God.*

The earth is the Lord's, and everything
in it, the world, and all who live in it; for
he founded it upon the seas and
established it upon the waters.

Psalms 24:1,2

The Bible is God revealing Himself to mankind.

Billy Graham is right when He says of the Bible: "The Bible is old; yet it is ever new. It is the most modern book in the world today. There is a false notion that a book as ancient as the Bible cannot speak to the needs of modern man. Men somehow think that in an age of scientific achievement, when knowledge has increased more in the past 25 years than in all preceding centuries put together, this ancient Book is out of date. But to all who read and love the Bible, it is relevant for our generation.

"It is in the Holy Scriptures that we find the answers to life's ultimate questions: Where did I come from? Why am I here? Where am I going? What is the purpose of my existence?"

The word "bible" comes from the Greek word "biblos," meaning book. But the Bible is more than a book—or a collection of books. It is God's written revelation of His will to men. Behind and beneath this book, above and beyond this book, is the God of the Book. For the Bible is all about God—and especially it is about God's Son, Jesus Christ.

MORE THAN A BOOK

The Bible contains 66 books, written by 40 authors, covering a period of approximately 1600 years. These authors came from all walks of life and included kings, peasants, prophets, poets, fishermen, statesmen, scholars, a businessman, a doctor and a missionary. It is separated into two major sections, the dividing place being the birth of Jesus Christ.

The first section is called the Old Testament. This portion was written mostly in Hebrew (with the exception of a few short passages in Aramaic) and was completed almost 400 years prior to the birth of Christ. The New Testament was written in the Greek language. Our present day English Bibles are all translated from these original languages.

The word "testament" actually means "covenant," or agreement. The Old Testament is a record of God's covenants with man—and points toward the coming of God's Son, Jesus. The New Testament is the record of the fulfillment of that covenant agreement through Jesus Christ.

WHO IT IS ABOUT

In the sign language for the deaf, the sign for Jesus is to point to the palms of both hands with the index finger of the other hand. This is symbolic of the nail prints in the hands of Jesus.

The sign for the Bible is to point with first one index finger then the other to the palms of both hands, then to open the palms up as if they were a book. In other words, the Bible is a book about Jesus Christ.

Several years ago I was visiting in Hong Kong and rode the hydrofoil from Hong Kong across the harbor to the tiny Portuguese colony of Macao. There, on a hill overlooking the harbor of Macao, the Portuguese once built a massive cathedral. Several centuries ago a typhoon proved stronger than the work of man's hands, and the huge, stone building fell in ruins. However, the front wall of the old cathedral still stands, with its wide steps leading down to the ancient cobblestone street bordering the harbor. High on top of that jutting wall, challenging the elements down through the years, is a great bronze cross.

In 1825 Sir John Bowering sailed his ship into Hong Kong harbor and caught a glimpse of that great cross, towering above the ruins of the old cathedral of St. Paul. Sir John was deeply moved. Retiring to the cabin of his ship, picking up a quill, he dipped it in ink and wrote these words in his journal.

> In the cross of Christ I glory
> Towering o'er the wrecks of time.
> All the light of sacred story
> Gathers round its head sublime.

The central message of the Bible is the cross of Jesus Christ. Every book of the Bible either points forward to the coming of Jesus, or points backward toward His work on Calvary.

There is a marvelous story in the book of Luke about an event that took place eight days after Jesus was born. His mother, Mary, and Joseph had taken the tiny baby to the Temple in Jerusalem so He could be circumcised according to the Jewish law. When they entered the Temple they were spotted by an old rabbi, a godly man named Simeon, who had been studying the Old Testament all his life. By reading the Bible he had become convinced that the central message of the Old Testament was to point toward the coming of the

Messiah—God's Son. In fact, the Holy Spirit had told him he would not die until he had seen the Saviour with his own eyes.

That day, when Mary and Joseph entered the Temple court carrying their tiny baby, something sparked in the old man's heart. He rushed forward, tears in his eyes, and asked Mary if he could hold the baby for just a moment. Taking the tiny child in his arms he gazed down on the face of Jesus. Then, turning his face heavenward he prayed:

"Sovereign Lord, as you have promised, you now dismiss your servant in peace. For my eyes have seen your salvation, which you have prepared in the sight of all people, a light for revelation to the Gentiles and for glory to your people Israel" (Luke 2:29-32).

Then Simeon said something very significant. *"This child is destined to cause the falling and rising of many in Israel, and to be a sign that will be spoken against, so that the thoughts of many hearts will be revealed."* Then looking deep into the tender eyes of the young mother the old man said, *"And a sword will pierce your own soul too."*

Simeon was referring to the Messianic prophecies he had been reading in the Old Testament—the prophecies which foretold the coming of the Son of God. In particular he was referring to a prophecy in Genesis when God said to the serpent, Satan, in the Garden of Eden, *"I will put enmity between you and the woman, and between your offspring and hers; he will crush your head, and you will strike his heel"* (Genesis 3:15). He also made reference to a prophecy by Isaiah, 700 years before the birth of Christ: *"I will make you a light for the Gentiles, that you may bring my salvation to the ends of the earth"* (Isaiah 49:6).

This is what the Lord says: "Let not the wise man boast of his wisdom or the strong man boast of his strength or the rich man boast of his riches, but let him who boasts boast about this: that he understands and knows me, that I am the Lord, who exercises kindness, justice and righteousness on earth, for in these I delight," declares the Lord.

Jeremiah 9:23,24

GOD'S DREAM

From the very beginning God had a dream. The dream was for man to be restored into full fellowship with God. Jesus was the answer to that dream. All the godly men across the ages who wrote the Bible picked up snatches of that dream—and included them in their writings. Therefore, throughout the Bible—from the time of Creation until the birth of Christ—you find the biblical writers referring to this Messianic dream. Jesus, then, is the central theme of the Bible.

Abraham saw His reflection in Melchizedek, King of Salem.

Jacob called Him Shiloh.

To Moses He was the Passover Lamb and the Lifted Up One.

To Joshua He was Captain of Our Salvation.

Ruth saw Him as Kinsman-Redeemer.

Samuel portrayed Him as Our King.

David called Him Lion of Judah and the Good Shepherd.

To Solomon He was the Beloved.

Ezra and Nehemiah pictured Him as our Restorer.

To Esther He was Our Advocate.

Job said He was my Redeemer.

Isaiah described Him as a suffering servant.

Jeremiah saw Him at the potter's wheel.

Ezekiel called Him the Son of Man.

Daniel called Him the Prince and the Smiting Stone.

CHAPTER FIVE

Hosea likened Him to a bridegroom redeeming a fallen wife.

To Joel He was the Restorer.

Amos saw Him as a Heavenly Husbandman.

To Obadiah He was Savior.

Jonah saw Him as Resurrection and Life.

Micah called Him a Witness.

To Nahum He was a Stronghold in a Day of Trouble.

Habakkuk described Him as God of My Salvation.

To Zephaniah He was a Jealous Lord.

Haggai said He was The Desire of All Nations.

Zechariah called Him the Righteous Branch.

Malachi declared Him the Sun of Righteousness.

And John the Baptist cried out: "Behold the Lamb of God who takes away the sin of the World."

As you read through the Old Testament there looms on the horizon of history One Person through whom God would establish His Kingdom on earth: Jesus Christ. Micah said He would be born in Bethlehem. Isaiah said He would be born of a virgin and would be called Emmanuel. David and Isaiah told how He would die and Job prophesied of His resurrection. Others pointed out He would be introduced by a strange prophet like Elijah, that He would work miracles, speak in parables, be rejected by leaders, be a smitten shepherd, a man of sorrows, would enter Jerusalem riding on a colt, would be betrayed by a friend for 30 pieces of silver and would be led as a lamb to the slaughter. He would die with the wicked. His hands and feet would be pierced. Not a bone of His body would be broken. Lots would be cast for His garments. He would be in the tomb three days, would rise from the dead and would ascend to Heaven at God's right hand.

It was foretold by David, Isaiah, Daniel, and Jeremiah that the Messiah would offer a new covenant for His people. He would send the Holy Spirit. His kingdom would be of the Gentiles and would be universal and endless.

All of this was written hundreds of years before Christ's birth, at which time the angels appeared to the shepherds on the hillside saying they had good tidings of great joy.

THE MIRACLE OF COMPOSITION

Suppose one man from each nation in the earth were to work a lifetime carving a tiny piece of marble. One day all these men, none of whom had ever met or even known anyone else was carving marble, would all gather in a small village in the hills south of Jerusalem—each one bringing their tiny piece of marble with them. The man who had carved what looked like a big toe would place his little piece on the ground. Then the man who had carved feet without toes or heels would attach his pieces—and they would fit perfectly. More toes would be added, each just the right size and shape. Then the man with the heels would attach his pieces. Then the ankles, the legs, the knees—each piece fitting so perfectly not even a seam showed—until the entire statue was completed, perfect in every detail.

How could such a statue be accounted for unless there was someone with a blueprint who had outlined to each man exactly what he was to carve?

No wonder the angels sang of "good tidings and great joy." The Miracle of the Ages, the One the Bible is all about, had been born in Bethlehem!

Remember, God's Word is the foundation of all we know about God—and of His plan for mankind. It tells of the origin of sin and how his curse separated man from God. Even though it contains the Law of God given to Moses on Mt. Sinai, we also discover how utterly impossible it was for the law to bring man the salvation he needs. Thus we find in its pages that the one purpose of God is to prepare the way for the coming of the Redeemer of the World, Jesus Christ.

Although the Bible is a library of books, it is also "the Book." It is a story, a grand story, of God's love for His people, and the price He was willing to pay to restore us into perfect fellowship with Him. While it is divine, it is also human. The thought is divine, the expression of the communication is human.

So here we have a book unlike all others. The Book, a divine revelation, a progressive revelation, a revelation of God to man communicated through men, that moves on smoothly from its beginning to its great end. Behind each event stands God, the builder of history, the maker of the ages. Eternity bounds the one side, eternity bounds the other side, and time is in between. You can study the minutest detail everywhere and see that there is one great purpose down through the ages—the eternal design of our Mighty God to redeem a wrecked world and give each of us—you and me—power for living.

The Old Testament is the account of God dealing with a nation—the Israelites. The New Testament is an account of God dealing with a Man—His Son. The nation was founded in order to bring the Man into the world.

God became man in the presence of His Son so we might know what God is like. If you want to know what God is like, look at Jesus, for He is the perfect revelation of God. His appearance on earth still marks the central event of all history. Even today's calendars are dated from that special time. The Old Testament set the stage. The New Testament describes the play.

And what a marvelous play it is. God is the author. Jesus Christ is the central character. The Holy Spirit is the power behind each of the characters—including the Son of God.

Jesus was a perfect man. He was kind, tender, gentle, patient and full of love. He worked miracles to feed the hungry, heal the sick, and raise the dead. Multitudes came to Him and He taught them about the Kingdom of God. But He threatened the religious people of the day—and eventually they killed Him. Yet even this had been foretold. It was necessary; for Jesus became the perfect sacrifice for our sins. By His atoning death the way was opened for all mankind to once again have fellowship with the Father.

Then, the greatest of all miracles—Jesus rose from the dead! He is alive today. He is not merely an historical figure, but a living Person—the most important fact of history, and the most vital force in the world.

His friends and followers wanted Him to remain on earth after His resurrection from the dead. But He said He had to leave. He had to leave so He could send His Holy Spirit. That Spirit, He said, the same Spirit who gave Him power to rise from the dead, would come and fill each Christian from that time on—giving them power for living. Several years ago I spent time with a young woman who had been part of the Charles Manson gang. She had been convicted on seven counts of first degree murder and sentenced to die in the California gas chamber. Shortly before she was to be executed, her sentence was changed to life in prison. During that time she received Jesus Christ as her Lord and Saviour. She had subsequently led a number of young women in prison into a salvation experience with Jesus Christ.

When I heard about this I sought and received permission to visit her in her cell at the California Institution for Women near Chino. We became good friends during these visits, for she had truly been "born again" and was a child of God.

On one of these visits she told me how she had received Christ. The first week after she arrived in prison, she received a Bible through the mail. She tossed it to one side and didn't even look at it for more than a year. But unknown to her a large number of people were praying for her. She received several letters from strangers, telling her about God's forgiving love. Then one day she took the Bible off the shelf in her little cell, brushed the dust off the cover, and settled back to read. Knowing virtually nothing about the Bible (although she had attended Sunday school as a child), she began to read—starting with the first page.

It was tough reading, but she was determined to find out what the Bible was all about. When she got to the book of Exodus and read the story of the Children of Israel, she became angry. Here was the story of God's love and provision. He delivered the Israelites from captivity in Egypt, opened the sea so they could escape, protected them from harm, provided water from rocks and manna every morning. Still the people griped and complained. Why, she asked herself, would anyone who was loved as much as God loved the Israelites refuse that love and respond so selfishly?

She read on through the Psalms—those beautiful love songs by David. Time after time she had to put the Bible down because tears filled her eyes. All she had ever known from childhood was hate. That was why she joined the Manson gang and participated in those horrible murders. Now she was reading about a tender, loving Heavenly Father. She had never known such love existed.

The books by the prophets all told her of a Saviour—one who would take away her sin and give her power for living. But they didn't tell her how to find Him—just that He was coming.

In the Gospels she read the life story of Jesus. He was all she imagined Him to be—loving, tender, kind, yet a man of justice and righteousness. It was what she had longed for all her life. She read on through the book of Acts and saw how those early Christians, full of the Holy Spirit, had gone out and performed the same miracles Jesus performed. How she longed for that same power in her life. It wasn't until she finally reached the last book in the Bible that she discovered how she could be forgiven of her sins and receive power for living.

Reading through the book of Revelation, she came upon the words of Jesus, an invitation she sensed was given just to her.

"Those whom I love I rebuke and discipline. So be earnest, and repent."

She paused in her reading, letting the words sink in. Could it be she was in prison not because she was a murderer, but because God loved her and was waiting for her to repent so He could give her power for living?

She read on. *"Here I am! I stand at the door and knock. If anyone hears my voice and opens the door, I will go in and eat with him, and he with me. To him who overcomes, I will give the right to sit with me on my throne, just as I overcame and sat down with my Father on his throne"* (Revelation 3:19-21).

With tears streaming down her face, she slipped off her cot in her lonely prison cell and knelt on the concrete floor. The Son of God was knocking at the door of her heart, asking to come in. Even though she was a murderer He was waiting for her to repent and ask His forgiveness. She opened the door of her heart and prayed a simple prayer. "Come in, Lord Jesus, take over my life."

Susan Atkins is still in prison, but she is a free woman. She has been set free by the Son of God. She has found new life right where she is—and she has received power to live that life through Jesus Christ.

The Bible, to Susan Atkins, was more than an ancient book. It was—and is—the Book of Life.

But his delight is in the law of the Lord,
and on his law he meditates day and
night. He is like a tree planted by
streams of water, which yields its fruit in
season and whose leaf does not wither.
Whatever he does prospers.

Psalms 1:2,3

MAKING THE BIBLE A PART OF YOUR LIFE

Suppose you are planning a trip. You carefully pack your suitcase, perhaps suspend your newspaper delivery, even get your car checked and gather your family to go with you. You attend to every necessary detail except one: you never pick up a road map.

Because you're in a hurry to reach your destination, you jump in your car and start driving. Which direction do you go: north, east, south or west? Does it make any difference?

Since you feel you're headed the right way, you keep on driving. You are like the bus driver who after a day of hard driving turned to his passengers and said, "Folks, I have good news and bad news.

"The bad news is we're lost and I haven't the faintest idea where we are. The good news is we're making excellent time!"

A lot of people start out on their Christian journey this way. They are so excited about their progress they get lost along the way. They are so intent on reaching their destination they ignore the basic steps they should take to get there. In other words, they ignore the fundamental Instruction Manual, the Word of God, which has the principles by which we live and die.

In this chapter I want to give you some practical, helpful hints on Bible study—which will make the journey much easier.

WHERE DO YOU START?

First, everything you need to know about power for living is found in this Book. In its pages are God's instructions on how to raise your family, how to treat your wife or husband, how you should eat, how you should worship... in short, everything you need to know about money, work, fear, pain, sex, and death. Any problem you can experience has its solution in the Bible.

Start by recognizing that even though the Bible is an entire library of 66 books—it is also one book. In Genesis you find the beginnings, in the Revelation you discover how it all winds up. And from Exodus (the 2nd book) to Jude (the next-to-last book) you see how God carried out His purpose. You cannot dispense with any part of it.

The Old Testament is the foundation; the New Testament is the superstructure. A foundation is of no value unless a building be built upon it. A building is impossible unless there is a foundation—and makes no sense unless there is a superstructure. Thus both Old and New Testaments are of equal value.

The Bible is one book, one history, one story. His story. Behind every event stands God, the builder of history, the maker of the ages.

In its original version the books of the Bible were not divided into chapters and verses. Each book was written to be read from beginning to end. God took great pains to give it to us as a progressive revelation of Himself, and you should take great pains to read it from beginning to end. You'll never understand it if you simply open it at random and begin reading.

This does not mean, however, that particular verses or chapters will not become especially meaningful to you. History is filled with stories of men and women who simply opened the Bible, and heard God speaking so profoundly it changed their lives. In the beginning, it may be too difficult to wade through long books and chapters. Verses and sections of verses, especially Psalms and Proverbs, will be meaningful to you regardless of the order in which you read them. This should never suffice, though, for earnest, systematic study of the Bible as a complete unity. Just as you would never dream of going to the library, checking out a book, and begin reading in the middle, so you need to learn to view the Bible as one book.

A LOVE STORY

The Bible is the greatest love story ever written. It is the story of God's love for all mankind—especially you. It is not a book of verses such as you would find on greeting cards; it is a revelation. It must be read, digested, studied, questioned and revered from beginning to end. Don't divide it into short devotional paragraphs and think you can understand its message. Come to its pages with common sense, believe that every book is about something and read and reread until you find out what that book is about.

Since the Bible was inspired by the Holy Spirit, you need the Holy Spirit's power to help you understand it, to interpret it. That is one of the functions of the Holy Spirit— to help you understand the Bible. Therefore, before you begin any serious study of the Bible, ask the Holy Spirit to fill you. Only as He interprets it to you will it make any sense. Otherwise it will be nothing more than great literature, interesting history, or a jumble of words and genealogies.

Are all the books of the Bible of equal importance? No, but all are indispensable. If you were to ask me if my brain is more important than my hand, I would tell you my brain is more important. Yet my hand is important also—and I would have a difficult time without it. So with the Bible. Every book is necessary to make a perfect whole, but some portions are more precious than others. You can't take away the book of Esther or the Song of Solomon and have a perfect revelation of God. Yet no one says either of these two books is comparable with the Gospel of John, or the book of Exodus. All are part of an organism and that organism is not complete if any part is missing.

THE A,B,C's OF BIBLE READING

How, then, should we begin reading? Why not begin reading the same way you would visit an art museum. Walk with your guide down the long rows of pictures. What do you do? Well, for one thing you don't walk hurriedly. Nor do you carry on a conversation about the stock market or the world series with a friend. You listen carefully to your guide as he pauses in front of each picture. There he describes, not the picture, but the artist. He tells you who the artist was, what he was going through when he painted the picture, where he lived and what he was trying to express through his art. Then he talks about the various art forms. Some paintings are realistic, others are abstract. You need to understand the artist's techniques and style, how he used composition, lights, color, shadows and proportions. Then, finally, the guide will ask you to study the painting itself and see if it has a message for you as an individual.

That's the way you should study the Bible.

Begin With the Author

Studying the Bible is much like learning to interpret art. First, you should know the author of each book. As a writer I have learned, for instance, that those who understand my books best are those who know me. The better you know me the better you understand what I have written.

That's the reason you need to start with the Holy Spirit when studying the Bible. The Holy Spirit worked through every writer of these books, revealing the nature of God.

Then you need to learn as much as you can about the human writers. Amos, for instance, wrote the book that carries his name. It is helpful to know that Amos was a farmer, a herdsman, that he lived in a time when the Kingdom of Israel was divided into two nations—a southern and a northern kingdom, much like the United States was divided during the Civil War. Amos lived in the Southern Kingdom called Judah. When he prophesied against the northern kingdom he got a lot of "Amens!" from his southern audience. But when he began pointing out the sins of Judah, they ran him out of town.

Knowing this background helps in understanding the content of the book.

Take another case. It is helpful to know that the same man who wrote the Gospel of Luke also wrote the book of Acts. His name was Luke. He was a physician turned biographer. Not only did he write one of the four biographies of Jesus found in the New Testament, but he later traveled with the Apostle Paul and wrote the history of the early church—actually the biography of Paul in a book called Acts. When you discover that Luke was a medical doctor, you can understand why he uses certain language, his close attention to detail, and his many references to physical healings and miracles.

Each writer of the Bible—from Moses to the Apostle John—used a different style. But each was inspired by the Holy Spirit and all he wrote was true and without error. No one writer had a full picture of God, but when their writings are put together you see God in all His glory—in His entirety.

Select a Good Version of the Bible

There are many different versions of Bibles on today's market. Owning a Bible which is easy to read is important for the beginning reader. For years all we had to read was the Bible authorized by King James in 1611. It is a magnificent book with flowing poetic language which has blessed millions of people across the years. But in the 20th century, it is difficult to understand. It is full of "thees" and "thous" and uses many words which are no longer popular.

Most of the scripture used in this book is from the New International Version—which is my favorite. It is easy to read and correctly translated from the original languages.

Others prefer to start with one of the paraphrased translations such as *The Living Bible*. It is extremely easy to read. When used alongside one of the other newer translations, it makes Bible reading easy and exciting.

Read for the Big Picture

A good practice is to train yourself to read the Bible one book at a time. The first time you read a book in the Bible, try to get an overall feel for what the book says. This is the skyscraper view. Don't worry about details, try to get the panoramic sweep. It's like climbing into a tree to see everything from above.

Start, for instance, with the book of Mark. Mark is easy to read. It is an action book about the life of Jesus, full of stories without too much difficult teaching.

Or you may want to start with Genesis. It's the same kind of book, filled with wonderful history. You probably won't read Genesis all at one sitting, but you can read it by sections. I like to read Genesis as a book of people's lives. That is, I like to see it as a book of biographies of men like myself. So I read about Adam and Eve. Then about Noah. There is a long section about Abraham. Another about Isaac. And finally those thrilling stories about Jacob—who was a man so much like I am. When you view Genesis as a book of stories about people, it is not only easy, but exciting to read.

Do not start in the middle of the Bible with books like Daniel or Isaiah. They simply won't make sense until you begin to get the big picture.

Read for Details

Don't stop with first impressions. Now that you are looking at the Bible from the top of a skyscraper, move on down and get a sidewalk perspective as well. At this point it helps to begin to follow some steps.

(1) *Start by reading a book a week.* This is not as difficult as it sounds. The longest book in the Bible can be read by spending less than one hour a day. Simply divide the book into seven equal parts, set aside a special time each day to read, and establish a habit of Bible reading.

(2) *Use a notebook.* Don't just read. Make notes as you do. Underline passages in your Bible that seem significant to you and make notes in your notebook about any questions you may have, or any ideas the Holy Spirit may give you as you read.

I often use my notebook during Bible reading as I do when I pray. I make notes on what God is saying to *me.* After all, that's why we should be reading the Bible. It is more than God's Word. It is God's Word to ME. Well, if God is speaking to me I'd better take notes on what He is saying. So I nearly always read the Bible with an open notebook—pen ready to jot down God's personal message to me.

Perhaps the most meaningful Bible I have is the one my father used immediately after he received Jesus Christ as his personal Saviour and Lord at the age of 62. My father had always been a good man—an active member of the church. But it wasn't until he went through a deep, personal trauma that he surrendered his life to Jesus Christ. Immediately he began an intense study of the Bible. He wanted to know what God was saying to him. He began by using a modern translation. Not only did he read, but he underlined, using different colors for different emphasis, and he made many notes in the margins of the Bible. It is these notes, along with his exclamation points, question marks and stars which helped guide me through my own initial Bible study three years later when I, too, received Jesus Christ as my Saviour and Lord.

Writing does something for the mind. Simply putting thoughts on paper helps record them in your brain. I love to see people taking notes in church for future reference. I recommend you make notes directly on the pages of your Bible. When that Bible is full, go to another.

You also might want to record your personal *paraphrase* of the passage you're studying. How does it translate into *your* life? A paraphrase is rewriting the Scripture in your own words. You'll be astonished at the results. It will make you study aspects of the verse of which you weren't aware. Also, it will help you remember what the passage says.

(3) *Read devotionally.* I recommend you read the Bible seriously, as you would study a book. But in order to get the most out of the Christian life you should read it devotionally—believing God will give you hidden nuggets of gold as you dip your pan into its stream.

Let me give you an example of this in my life several years ago.

One day I was alone in our little cabin in the Blue Ridge Mountains of North Carolina. It was just a few weeks after my father had died. I had come to the cabin without my wife or children to work my way through my grief. One afternoon sitting in an old rocking chair on the front porch, looking out at the brilliant autumn colors sprinkled across the mountains, I opened my Bible to the Twenty-third Psalm—an old favorite. I read it through casually, but my eyes stopped and rested on verse four: *"Thy rod and thy staff they comfort me."*

The property where our mountain cabin is located had been developed by my father over the last 40 years. He had the land cleared, had a stone mason come in and build the rock wall beside the driveway, and had worked with our old friend and neighbor, Raymond Cox, to build the cabins. He loved this place and would come up during the hot summer months to escape the Florida heat. He also loved to come up in the autumn to sit on this porch, rock in this chair, and enjoy the beautiful colors of nature. Everywhere I looked I saw my father's signature on the property.

I glanced up from my Bible, blinking back the tears of grief, and saw—standing in the corner of the porch—my father's favorite walking stick. He had carved it out of a crooked rhododendron branch. Although it looked much like an Irish shillelagh, I saw it as something far more. I could still hear my father that day when I was a sophisticated sophomore in college—still far from the Lord. Daddy, who had surrendered his life to Jesus Christ the summer before, had finished carving and sanding on the walking stick. Holding it up for me to see, he grinned and said, "From this time on, every time you see this old stick, you will be reminded that it is God's rod and God's staff which brings you comfort."

Suddenly the grief was gone. In its place was the Presence of God.

Read devotionally, and let God meet you at your place of greatest need—perhaps through a simple verse and a small reminder at your elbow.

(4) *Ask questions.* The Bible is not so sacred that it cannot stand honest examination. Ask *when* a thing took place. Ask *why* it was included in the Bible. Ask *where* it happened. Ask *who* was writing, *who* it was written about and to *whom* was it written. Ask *what* it meant at that time and *what* should it mean to you. Don't be frustrated if your study raises more questions than you can answer. You are dipping into a great well of spiritual knowledge that has no limits but will quench all thirst.

(5) *Respond.* Bible study is not an end. It is the means to an end. Many people have studied, even memorized the Bible, but have not responded personally to its call on their lives. The reason we study the Bible is so we can discover God's will for our lives—and apply it. Your study will uncover many things God wants you to do. But unless you respond, all your Bible study will be meaningless.

I once read of a mule standing exactly between two identical hay stacks. He was extremely hungry, but the poor animal stood there and starved to death because it never could make up its mind from which stack to eat.

Often we find ourselves in the same position as that mule. We read the Bible and in it we find God's will for our lives. But since that will usually is in conflict with something else going on in our lives—we simply stand still where we are . . . and starve to death.

The Swedish Nightingale, Jenny Lind, whose real name was Goldschmidt, won great success as an opera singer. She was at one time the richest and most famous singer in the world. Then one day, at the height of her fabulous career, she left the stage and never returned—choosing to live in privacy.

One day an English friend found her sitting on the steps of a small beach cottage watching a magnificent sunset over the ocean. On her knee was an open Bible. They talked and eventually the English woman asked the inevitable question. "Madam Goldschmidt, how is it that you came to abandon the stage at the very height of your success?"

The famous singer answered quietly. "When every day it made me think less of this," she said, laying her hand on the Bible, "and nothing at all of that," and she pointed to the sunset, "what else could I do?"

Jenny Lind did more than read her Bible. She responded to its call on her life as well.

(6) *Memorize your Bible.* Nothing will make the Bible a part of you as much as memorizing verses. *"I have hidden your word in my heart,"* the Psalmist said, *"that I might not sin against you"* (Psalm 119:11). Remembering that Jesus Christ is the "Word," and it is His presence which keeps us from sinning against God, nevertheless memorizing Scripture and hiding it in our hearts keeps the Presence of Christ fresh.

Prisoners of war in North Vietnam brought back stories of how they had pieced together all the verses of scripture they had memorized to form a partial Bible. It was these verses which helped some of them make it through those horrible years of imprisonment.

My mother and father established a pattern of Bible memorization which they carried on for years—committing one verse a week to memory. I know others who memorize a verse a day. Some people choose to memorize entire chapters at a time. A friend keeps Bible verses, written on little cards, above the sun visor of his car. When he is waiting at a traffic light, he flips down the sun visor and works on his Bible memorization. I have another friend, a jungle pilot who flies missionaries over the vast expanses of the Amazon jungle in small airplanes. He studies his scripture cards as he flies. A famous Bible teacher testifies that memorizing portions of the Bible was the secret to his overcoming an "uncurable" learning disability. Another says memorizing passages from the Bible helped him overcome stuttering.

"Your word is a lamp to my feet and a light for my path," David said (Psalm 119:105). Hide it in your heart and it will bring inner light as well.

(7) *Use Bible helps.* There are a number of good books which will help you study the Bible. Keep in mind that no book about the Bible is as good as the Bible itself, but the use of study aids will make things easier. Here are some books which you will want to get to help you along.

Concordance. A concordance is a book that lists all the words of the Bible and all the places that word is used. For instance, let's say you remember there is a verse of scripture someplace in the Bible that talks about "the valley of the shadow of death." Go to your concordance and look up the word "valley" or the word "death" just as you would look up a word in the dictionary. You will then find several scripture references after each one. With "valley" you'll find a number of references. The Bible talks about a "valley of dry bones" in Ezekiel 37:1, about a "valley of decision" in Joel 3:14, and about the "Lily of the Valley" in Song of Solomon 2:1. But if you keep checking you'll find a reference to "the valley of the shadow of death" in Psalm 23:4.

I recommend you start with a simple English concordance such as *Cruden's Complete Concordance* to help you trace words in the Bible.

Bible Dictionary. A Bible dictionary is a cross between a dictionary and a one-volume encyclopedia. It is a collection of articles explaining places, people and other subjects of the Bible. One of the best is the *New Bible Dictionary.*

Commentaries. A commentary is a running explanation of the Bible chapter by chapter (sometimes verse by verse). It explains what the text is about. Commentaries come in many-volumed sets with comprehensive explanations of each verse of scripture, to the more simple one-volume kinds. A fine one-volume commentary is the *New Bible Commentary.*

Bible Aids. There are numbers of books about the Bible. I recommend you visit a good Bible and book store in your city and ask the clerk to show you around. You'll be amazed at the vast collection of books, Bible atlases, maps and study guides available. They may also recommend to you a good Bible correspondence course which you can enroll in as a more serious Bible student.

A final word is important. While it is good to read the Bible alone in a "quiet time," it is exciting to study it as part of a group. There are thousands, indeed tens of thousands, of Bible study groups around the nation. Many of these are part of Bible-believing churches. Studying the Bible as a member of a group allows you to have access to what the Holy Spirit is teaching others. It will also help keep you from developing wrong interpretations. Therefore, even though I recommend private Bible study as part of your daily life, I hope you will find a small group of people—either a Bible study group which meets some evening of the week or perhaps a Sunday school class in a nearby church—and begin studying together with others who are also eager to learn more about power for living through Bible study.

Above all, I hope you remember that it is not the Bible but the Author of the Bible with whom you need to have fellowship. It is said that Gainsborough, the artist, longed also to be a musician. He bought musical instruments of many kinds and tried to play them. Once when he heard of a great violinist who brought ravishing music from his instrument, Gainsborough bought the violin on which the master played so beautifully. Surely, he thought, if I have that wonderful instrument I will be able to play too. But he soon learned that the music was not in the violin, it was in the violinist.

There is an old story of two men who were called on, in a large classroom, to recite the Twenty-third Psalm. One was a published orator trained in speech technique and drama. He repeated the psalm in a powerful way. When he finished, the audience cheered and even asked for an encore that they might hear his wonderful voice again.

Then the other man, who was much older, repeated the same words—"The Lord is my shepherd; I shall not want..." But when he finished, no sound came from the large class. Instead, the people sat in a deep mood of devotion and prayer.

Then the first man, the orator, stood to his feet. "I have a confession to make," he said. "The difference between what you have just heard from my old friend, and what you heard from me is this: I know the Psalm, my friend knows the Shepherd."

That, my friend, is power for living.

Let your eyes look straight ahead, fix
your gaze directly before you. Make level
paths for your feet and take only ways
that are firm. Do not swerve to the right
or the left; keep your foot from evil.

Proverbs 4:25-27

SUMMING IT UP

The driveway from my house is dirt. Actually it is a combination of sand and clay we call "marl" in Florida. It winds through the tall pine trees in front of our house and emerges on the county road—which is also marl. However, if you turn left you will soon hit the pavement. The road continues for a mile and connects with another paved road which in turn takes you out to I-95. Once on I-95 you can drive all the way to the state of Maine on a limited access, four-lane highway.

If I pull out of my garage and head down my marl driveway I can honestly say I am on the way to Maine. That does not mean I have arrived at my destination. Nor does it mean I'll get there before anyone else. But though I am still a long way off, and far behind, I can still say I am on the way.

If I drive into the ditch which borders the county road in front of my house, and get someone to pull me out, I can still say I am on the way. However, if I stay in the ditch, or if I turn right when I hit the county road rather than left, then I cannot honestly say I'm on the way. Only as long as I'm moving in the right direction am I on the way.

As a Christian you have not arrived at perfection. There has been only one man to live the perfect life—only one man who was totally filled with the Spirit. A Christian, however, is one who has determined that the direction of his life will be toward Jesus Christ—not away from Him. As long as you have your face toward Jesus, no matter how far behind you are, no matter if your tires are flat, no matter if you stay in the ditch more than on the highway, you are still on the way.

If you've gotten this far in the book, then that is a good indication you're a good piece down the road—and much closer to your destination than when you started. You may not feel any closer. In fact, a lot of things may be going wrong in your life right now. That doesn't make any difference; if you have given your life to Jesus Christ and have allowed the Holy Spirit to fill you, you are heading rightly, no matter how imperceptible the progress.

There are some closing thoughts I want to leave with you.

In the first place, the Christian life is not free from temptation. Don't be fooled into thinking that if you were more like Jesus you wouldn't be tempted. Jesus was perfect and was tempted the same way we are. In *Pilgrim's Progress,* John Bunyan points out that even at the gate of heaven there is a pathway leading to hell. In other words, no one this side of glory ever reaches the point where he cannot make a wrong turn.

Also I would like to remind you the Christian life is never free from mistakes. The best of us spend a lot of time in the ditches of life. But as Charles Allen once pointed out, the difference between a sheep and a pig is this: When a sheep falls in a mudhole, it bleats to get out. When a pig falls in, he just lies there and wallows.

As one who has been on the road for a long time, I spend a lot of time pulling over to the side and saying to friends and strangers who are in a ditch, "Though you have fallen, you still can get up and start again."

That's the reason we have a Saviour—to save us from our sin.

A Christian is one who is determined that the way of Christ is the best way and who has fully committed himself to that way.

In the front of my Bible I have penned a reminder to myself. It says simply:

"I cannot turn back, for I have entered into an irrevocable contract with God. I have committed my life to Jesus Christ and He has given me eternal life."

I invite you, if you have not already done so, to join me on the road to God with Jesus Christ. Power for living is yours when you come to Christ. I urge you to do it now.

FOR FURTHER READING

BIBLE VERSIONS

King James Version (1611)

The most well-known English version of the Bible. Its literary quality is unsurpassed. We can hear its words echoed in literature, poetry, hymns, and anthems.

New American Standard Version (1963)

A modern translation of the Bible that seeks to give a word for word rendering of the original languages. An excellent study version of the Bible.

New King James (1982)

An attempt by a team of 119 Bible translators to retain the beauty and purity of the original *King James Version* while making the text more readable.

New International Version (1978)

A completely new translation of the Bible made by over a hundred scholars. The distinguishing characteristic of the *NIV* is its readability.

BIBLE HELPS

Every Christian should read the Bible in a systematic way every day. A good place to start is with *The Daily Walk*. Each day you are given a passage of Scripture to read with an overview of the passage's message. A brief application to present-day circumstances follows the overview. By following *The Daily Walk*, you will read the entire Bible in a year. A daily devotional guide designed especially for families with a similar format is called *Family Walk*. These can be ordered from Walk Thru the Bible Ministries, P.O. Box 80587, Atlanta, GA 30366.

Adams, Jay E. *What to Do on Thursday*. Grand Rapids, MI: Baker Book House, 1982. A handy guide on how to interpret and apply the Bible to everyday living.

Alexander, David and Patricia Alexander. *Eerdmans' Handbook to the Bible*. Grand Rapids, MI: Wm. B. Eerdmans Publishing Co., 1973. A fully illustrated reference book that will help the reader understand the Bible in its historical context.

Douglas, J. D. et al., eds. 2nd edition. *The New Bible Dictionary: Revised*. Wheaton, IL: Tyndale House Publishers, Inc., 1982. A comprehensive study of Bible words, theological topics, places, people, names, etc.

Guthrie, Donald et al., eds. *New Bible Commentary: Revised*. Grand Rapids, MI: Wm. B. Eerdmans Publishing Co., 1970. A one-volume commentary on the Bible put together by a team of scholars explaining every chapter in the Bible.

Strong, James. *The Exhaustive Concordance of the Bible*. Various publishers. Every word in the *King James Version* of the Bible is listed alphabetically with its corresponding verse. Hebrew and Greek dictionaries are included. A tremendous asset in locating forgotten verses.

Taylor, Kennedy. *The Living Bible*. Wheaton, IL: Tyndale House Publishers, 1971. This is a paraphrase of the Bible in everyday English. A paraphrast states in different language what he understands to be the original author's meaning. A paraphrase should never substitute for a translation.

Thomas, Robert L., et al., eds. *New American Standard Concordance of the Bible*. Nashville, TN: Holman Bible Publishers, 1981. A concordance based on the *New American Standard Version* of the Bible.

CHURCH HISTORY

Houghton, S.M. *Sketches from Church History*. Carlisle, PA: Banner of Truth Trust, 1980. A very readable and attractive historical presentation of how the Gospel of Jesus Christ affected the world.

Kuiper, B. K. *The Church in History*. Grand Rapids, MI: Wm. B. Eerdmans Publishing Co., 1964. Originally written as a textbook for Christian schools. Those unfamiliar with church history would do well to start with this book.

CHRISTIAN BELIEF

Blanchard, John. *Right With God*. Chicago, IL: Moody Press, 1971. A brief but thorough explanation of what it means to be a Christian.

Bridges, Jerry. *The Pursuit of Holiness*. Colorado Springs, CO: Navpress, 1978. Answers the basic questions that Christians have concerning their battle with sin.

Ferguson, Sinclair B. *Know Your Christian Life*. Downers Grove, IL: InterVarsity Press, 1981. A practical application of Biblical doctrines.

LaHaye, Tim. *The Battle for the Mind*. Old Tappan, NJ: Fleming, H. Revell Co., 1980. An explanation of the many ideas that influence us on a daily basis and shape our thinking.

CREDITS

BIBLE REFERENCES

With the exception of the following verses, all Scripture quotations are taken from the *Holy Bible: New International Version.* Copyright © 1978 New York International Bible Society. Used by permission from Zondervan Bible Publishers.

Page 12, 46   *The Living Bible,* copyrighted 1971 by Kenneth Taylor.

Page 36   *The King James Version* (1611).

TESTIMONIES

Appreciation to the following for permission to adapt material:

For Roger Staubach, Chuck Colson   Printed by permission from *Evidence That Demands a Verdict* by Josh McDowell. Copyright © Here's Life Publishers, Inc., 1972, 1979. All rights reserved.

For Julius Irving   Printed by permission from *Athletes in Action.* Copyright © Here's Life Publishers, Inc., 1981. All rights reserved.

For Wallace Johnson   Printed by permission from *Worldwide Challenge,* Copyright © Campus Crusade for Christ, Inc., 1978. All rights reserved.

OTHER SOURCES

Appreciation to Josh McDowell for permission to adapt material from his books, *Evidence That Demands a Verdict* and *Evidence Growth Guide: Part II* (Published by Here's Life Publishers, Inc., San Bernardino, California) and from *The Year of the Bible Official Reading Guide* © 1983 (Walk Thru the Bible Ministries, Atlanta, Georgia).

The Four Spiritual Laws appearing in Chapter 3 are printed by permission. © Campus Crusade for Christ, Inc. (1965). All rights reserved.

ILLUSTRATIONS